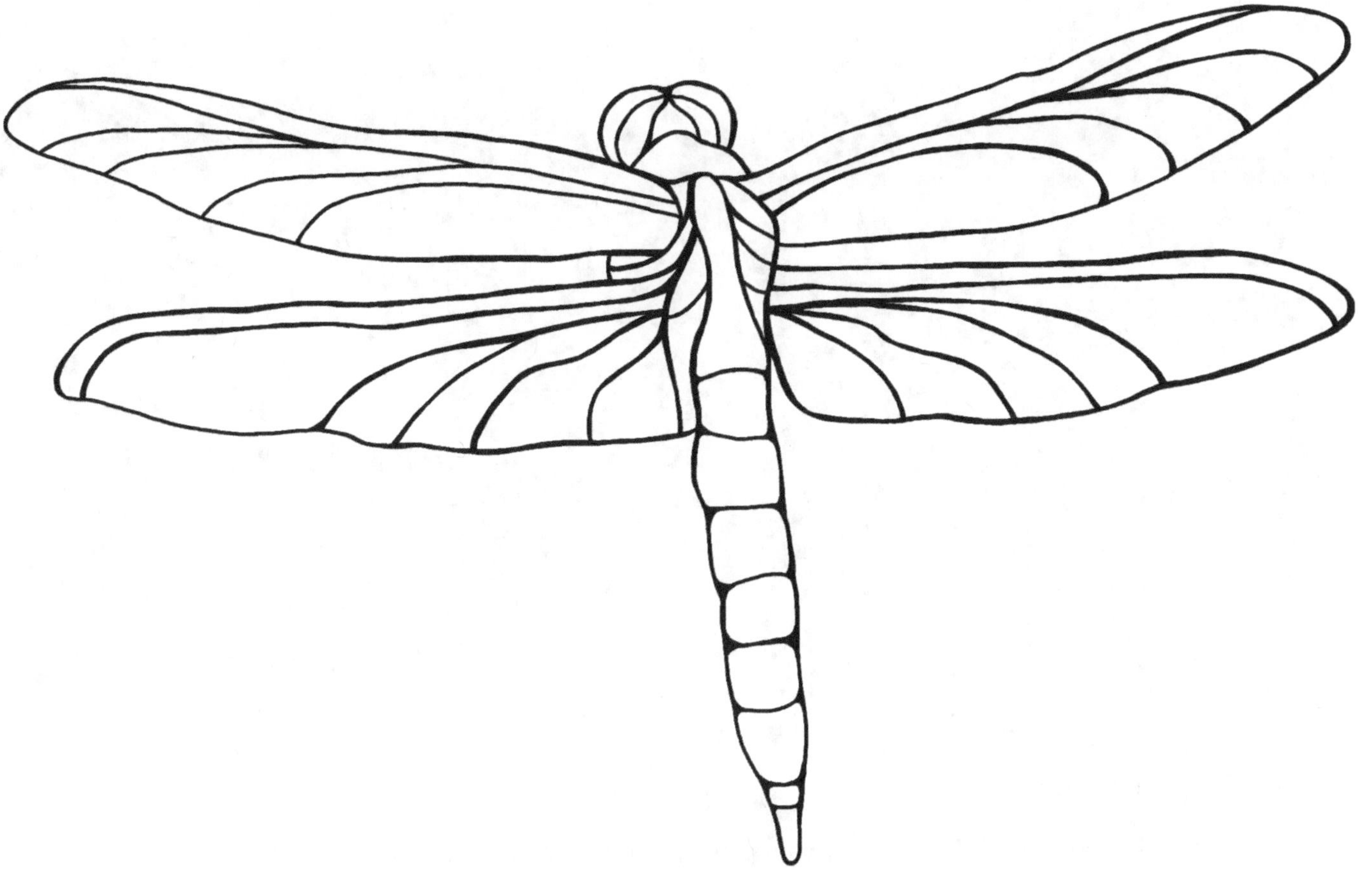

Magical Summer

Adult Coloring Book
30 Original Drawings

Magical Summer

Independently Published ISBN 978-1-79063-138-4

Cover design by K.M. Lynn, cover image by K.M. Lynn

All images are original art by K.M. Lynn

Published in the United States

Printed in the United States by CreateSpace

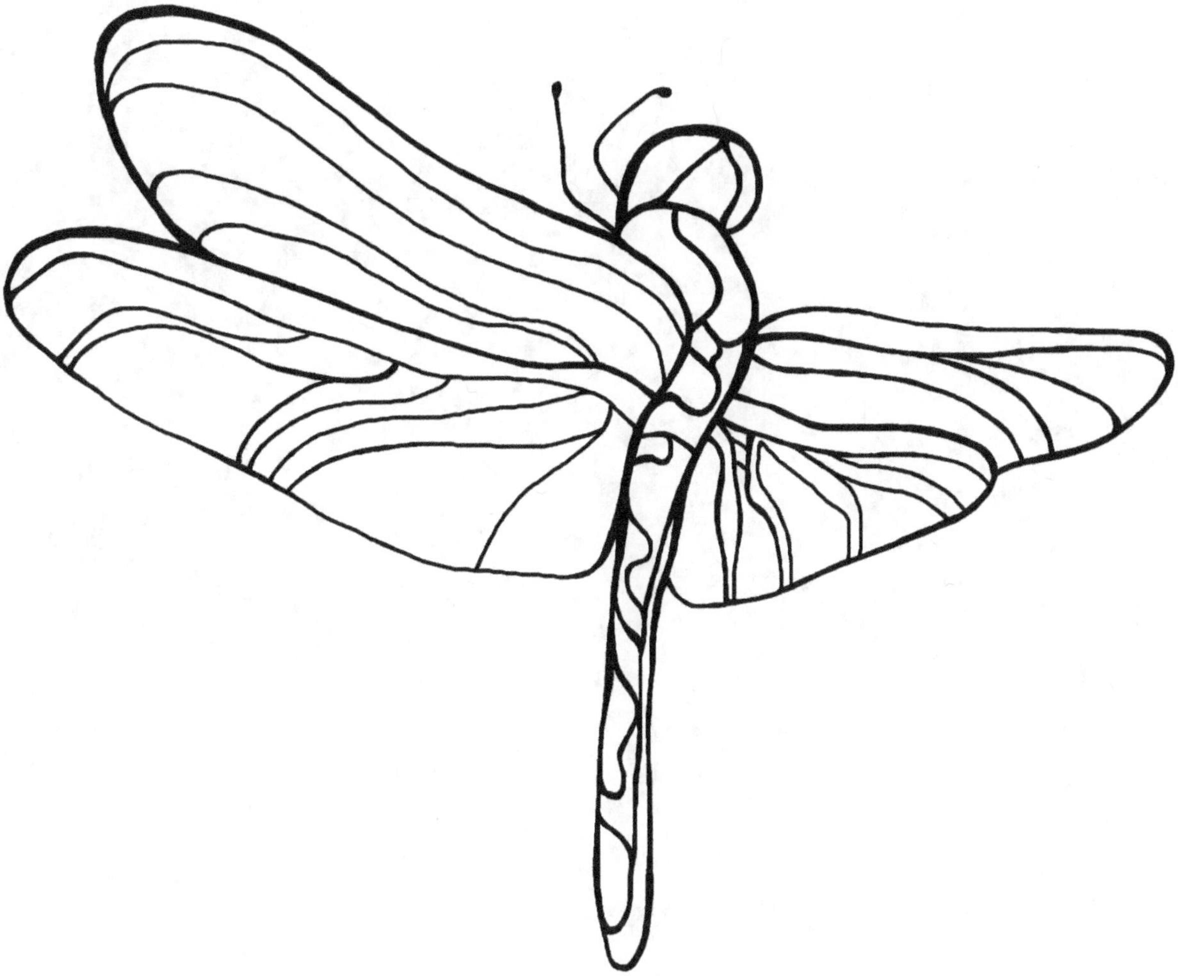

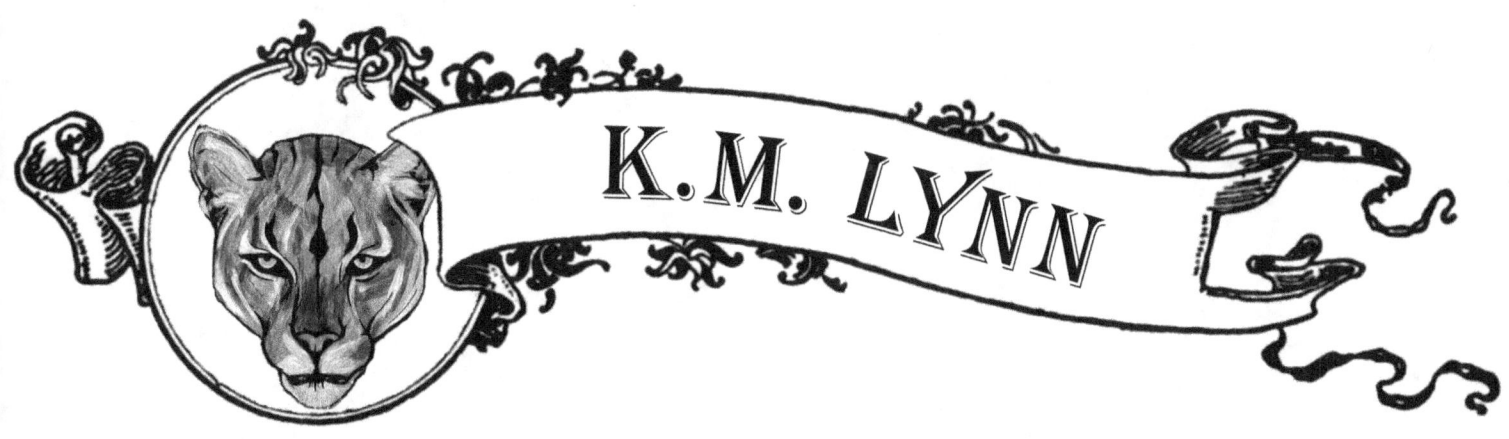

Oringal drawings lovingly created by

K.M. LYNN

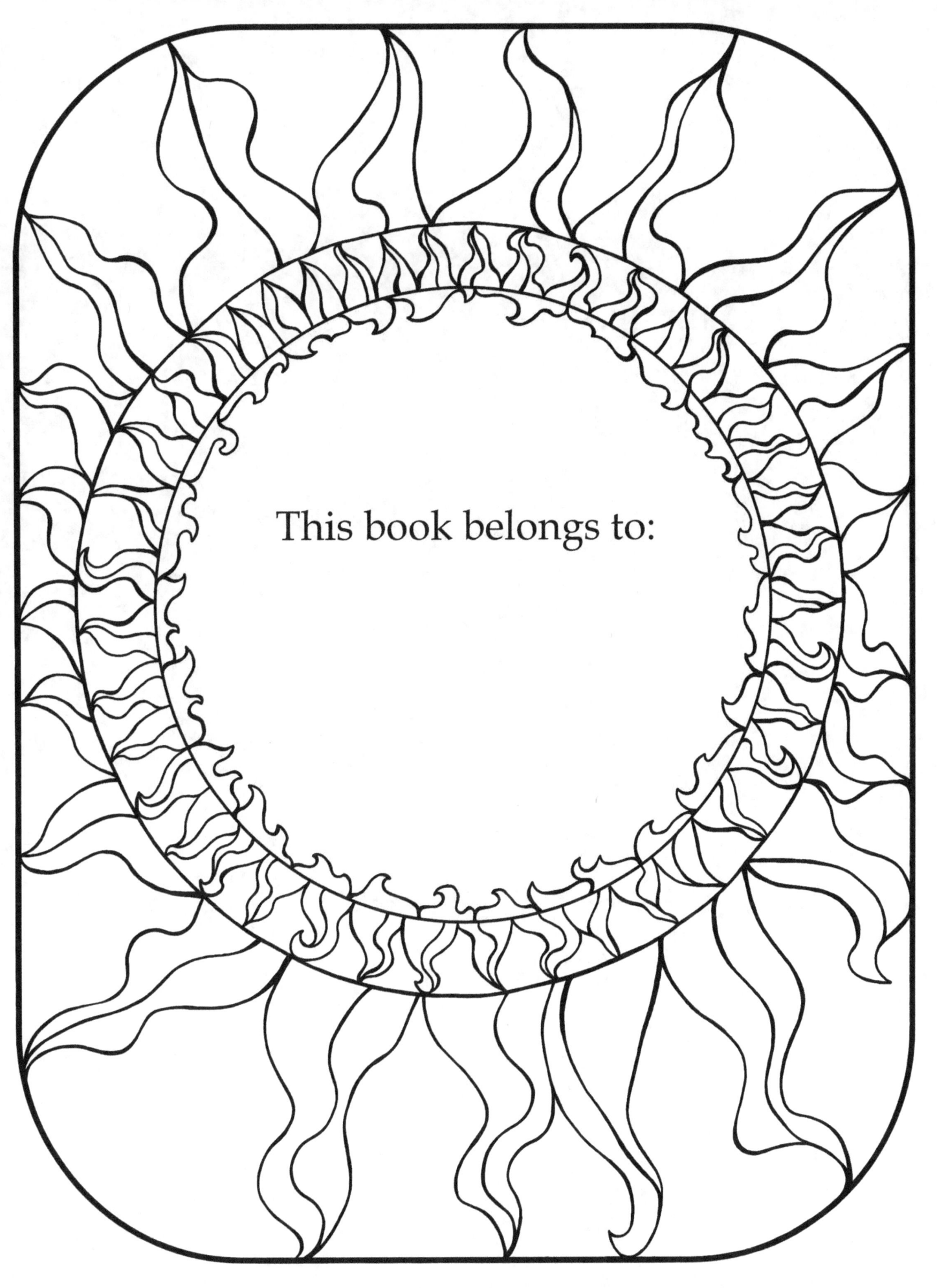

This book belongs to:

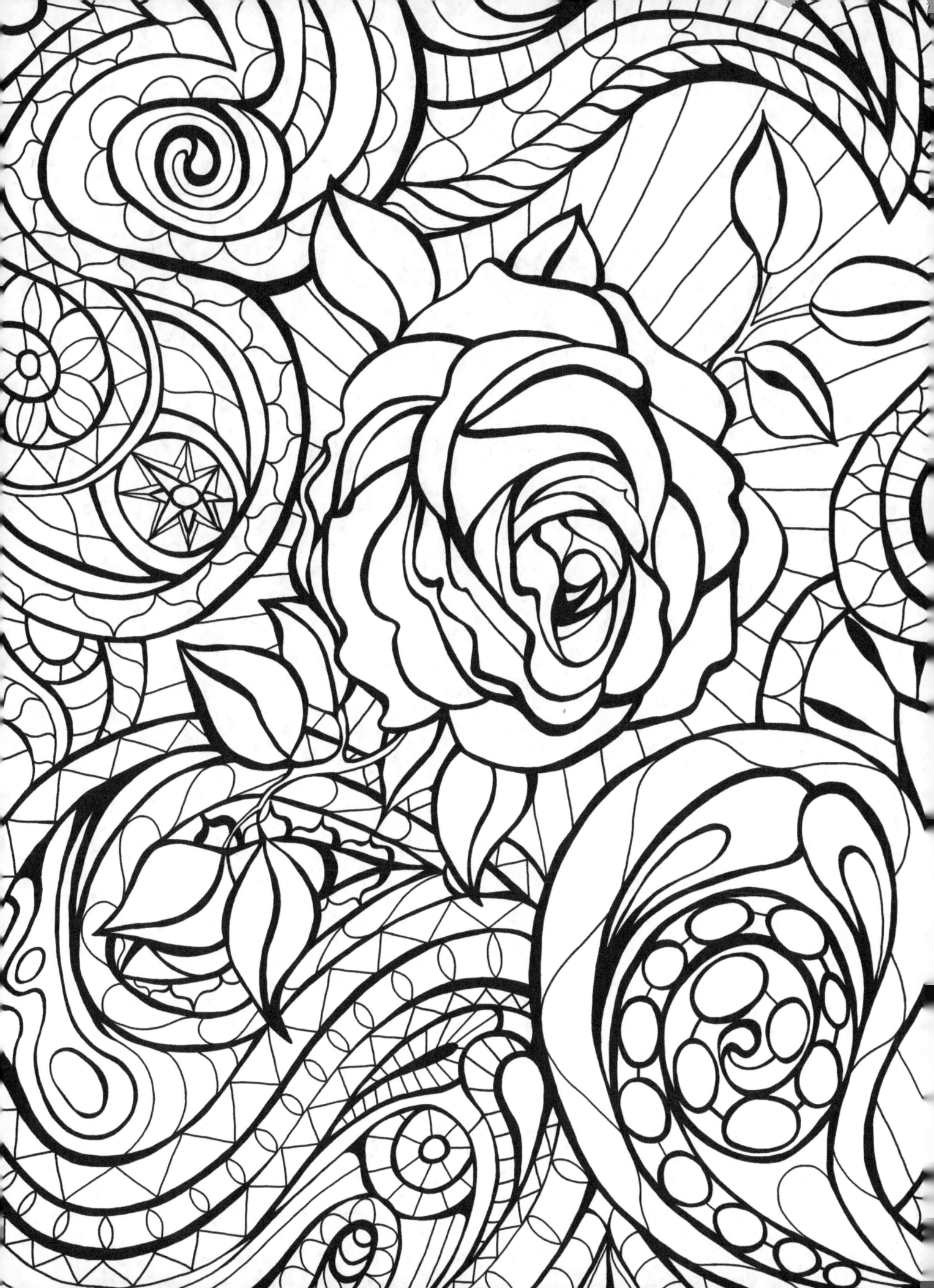

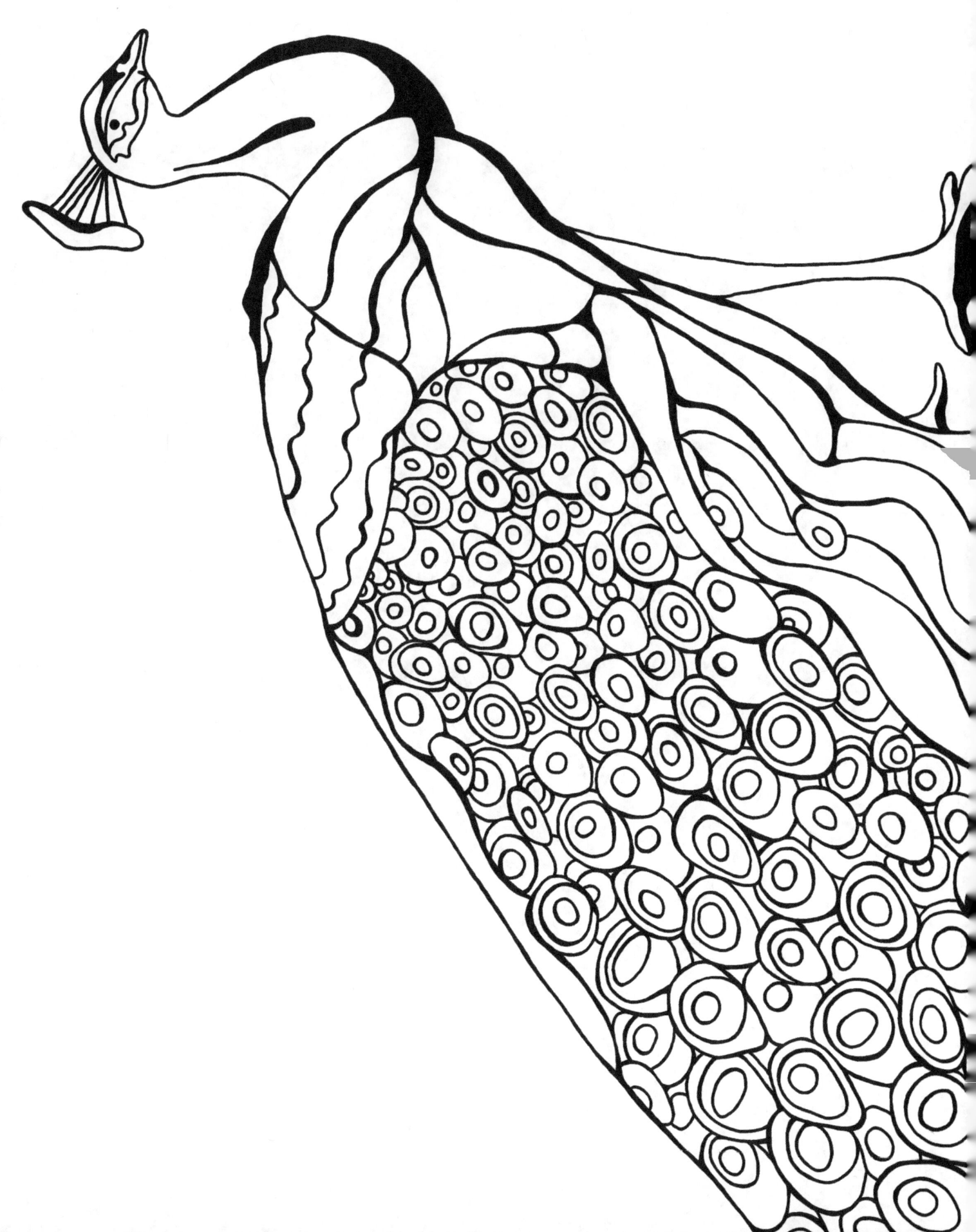

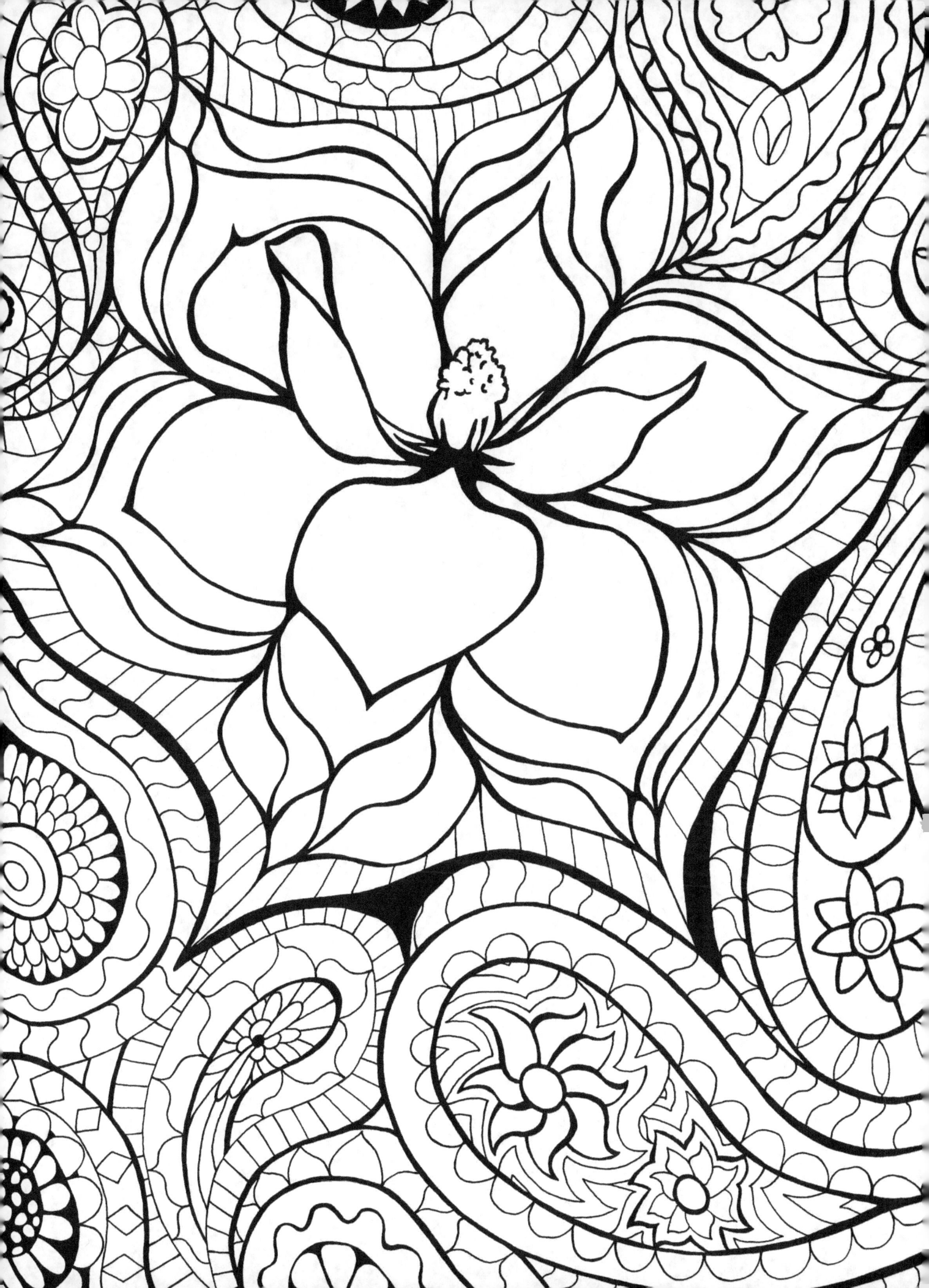

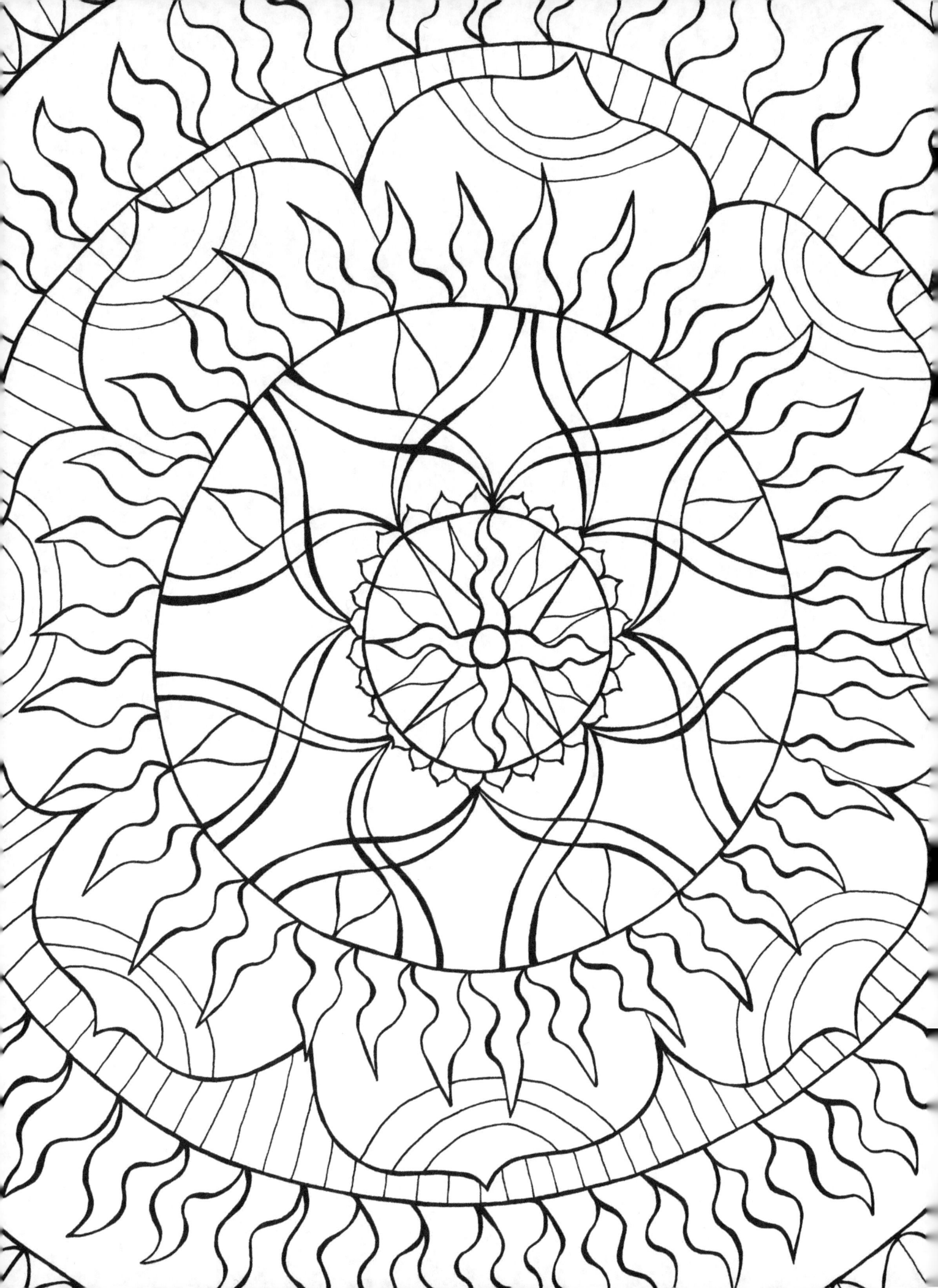

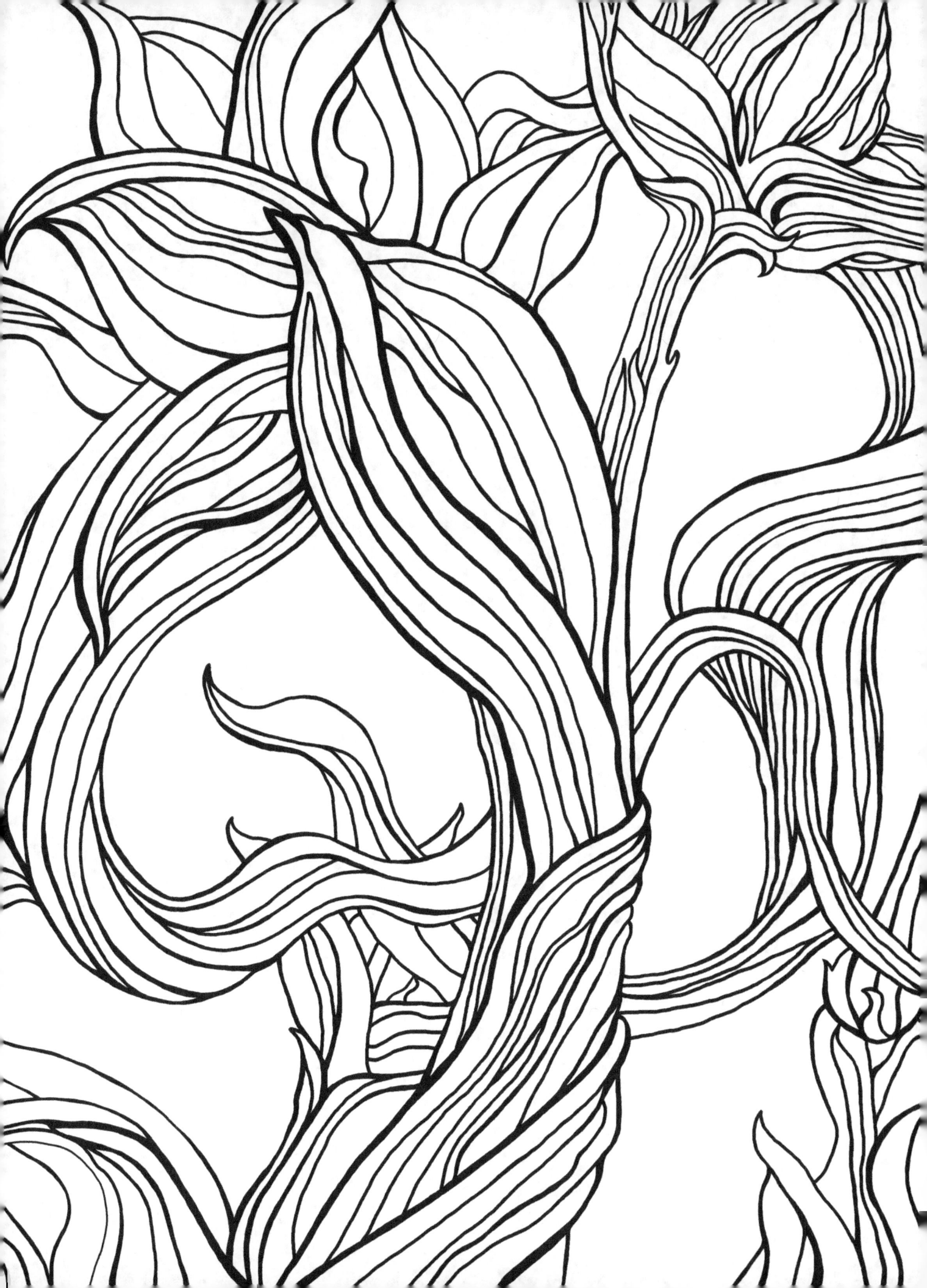

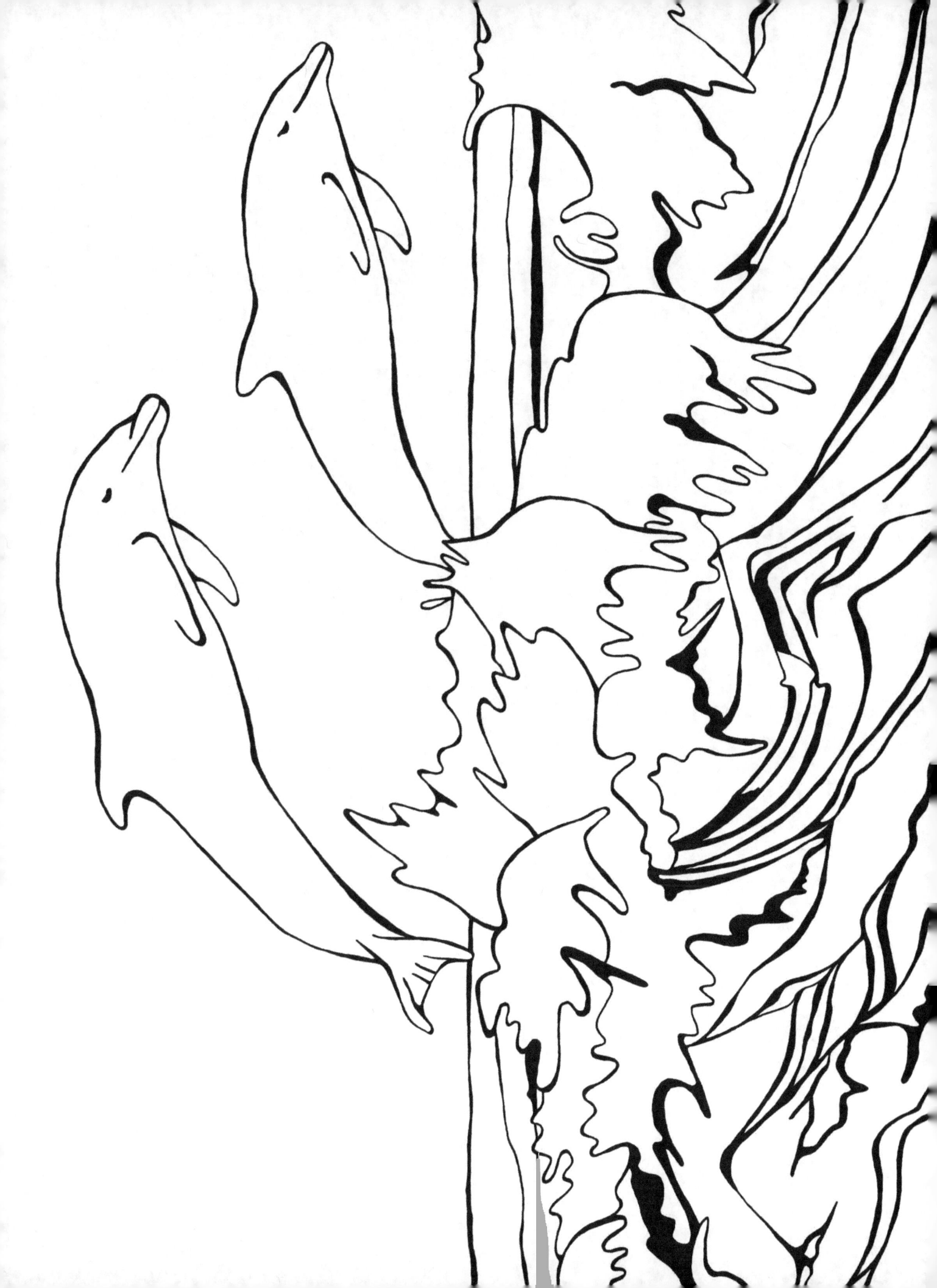

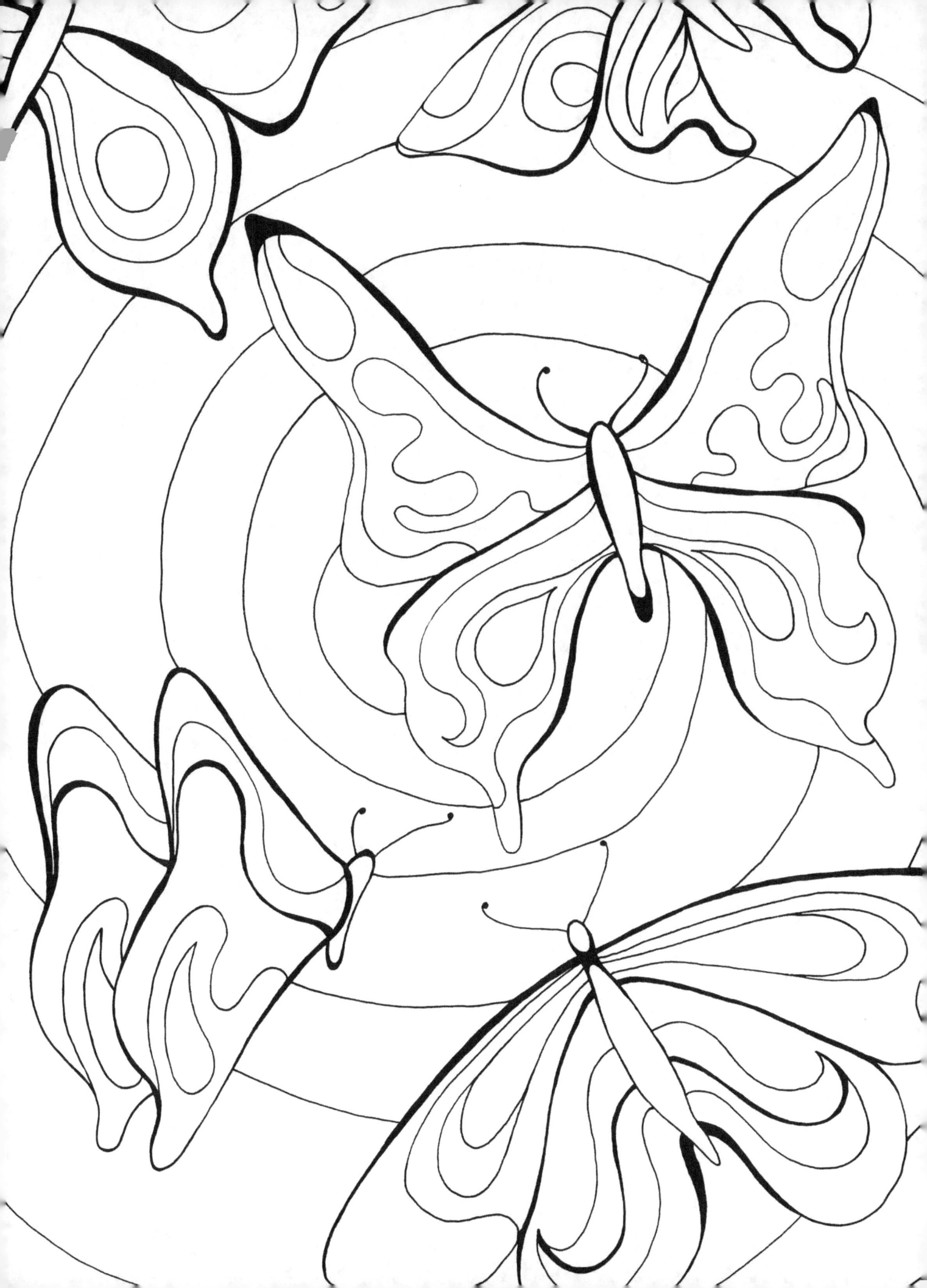

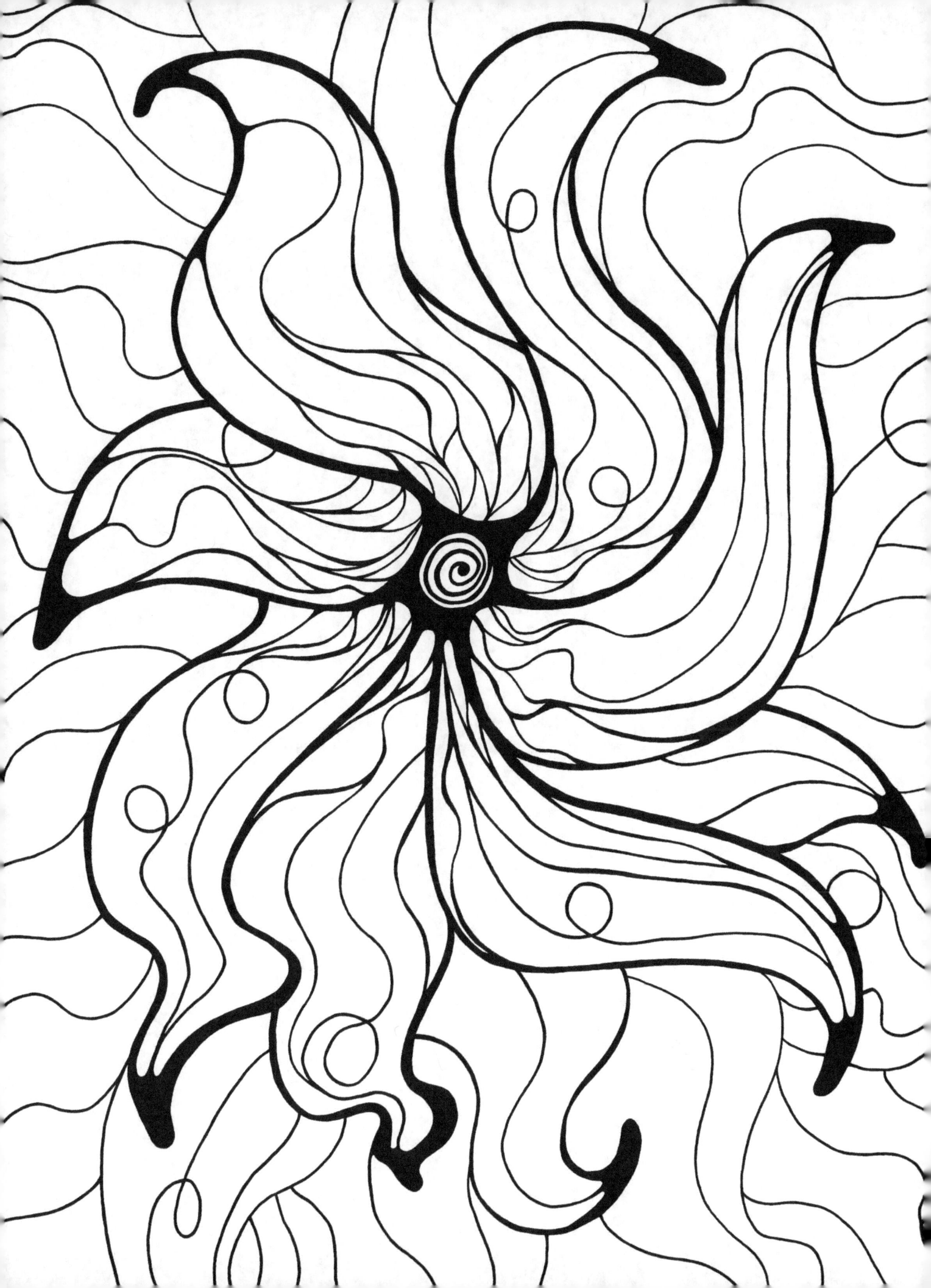

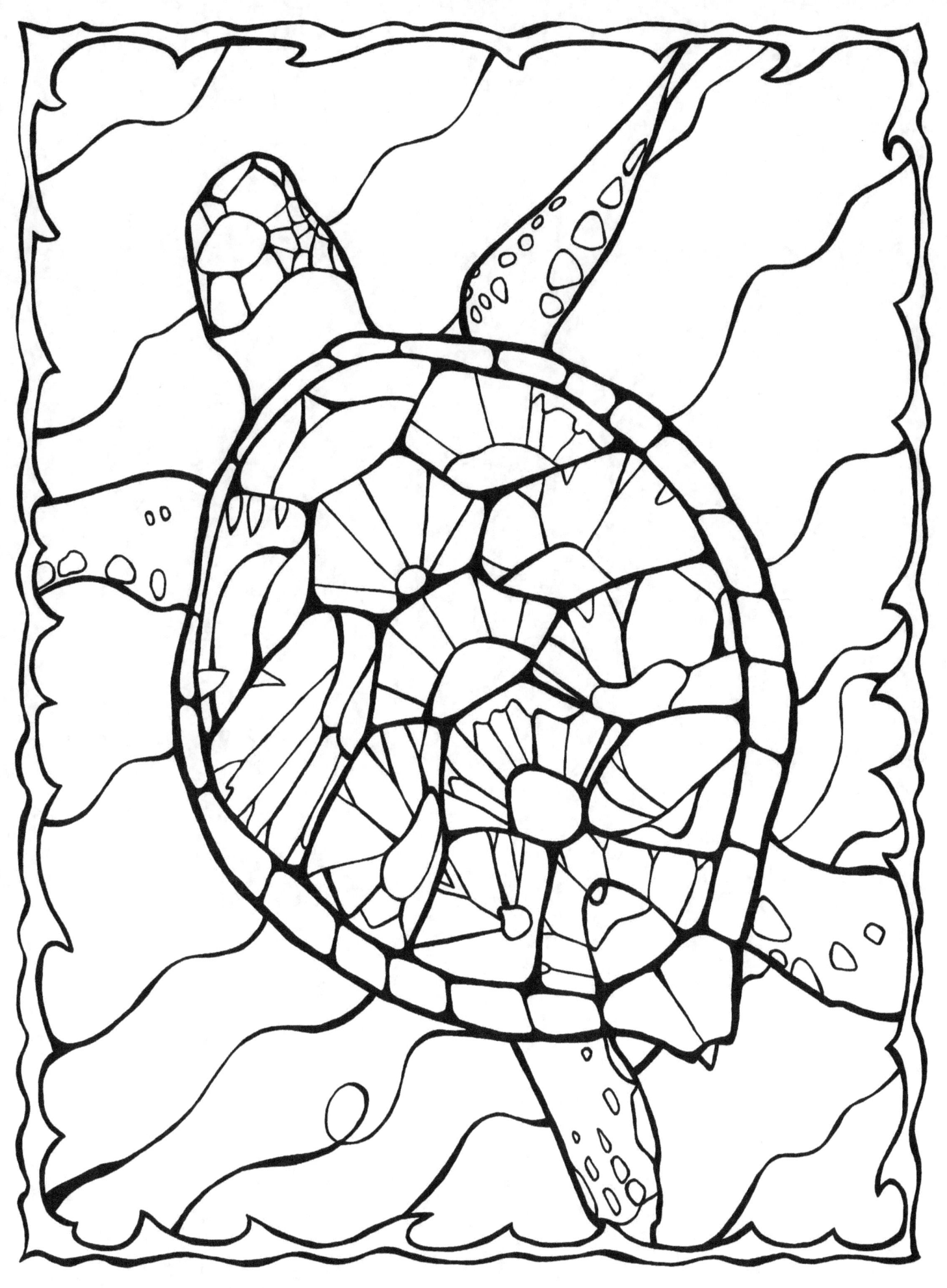

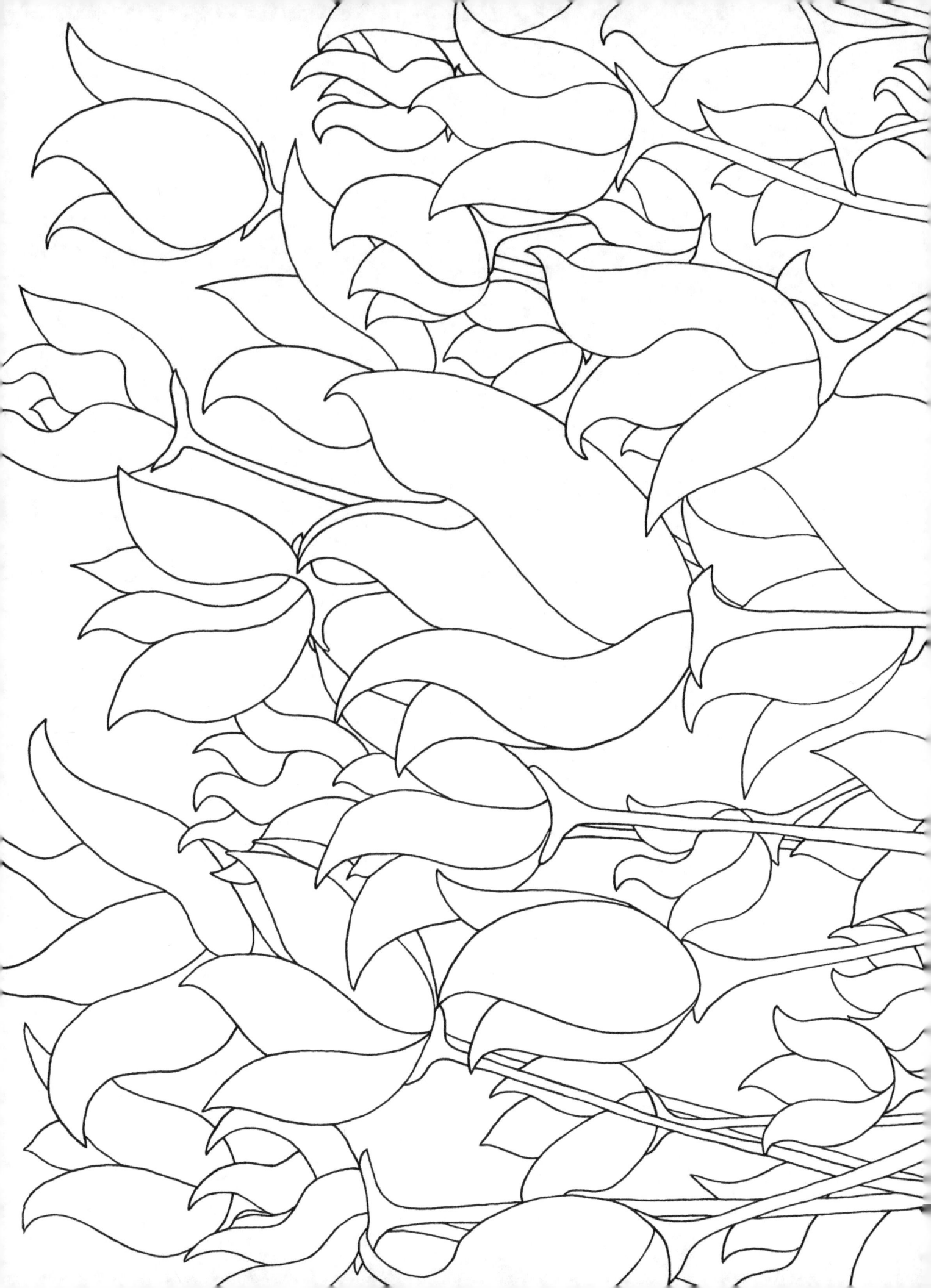

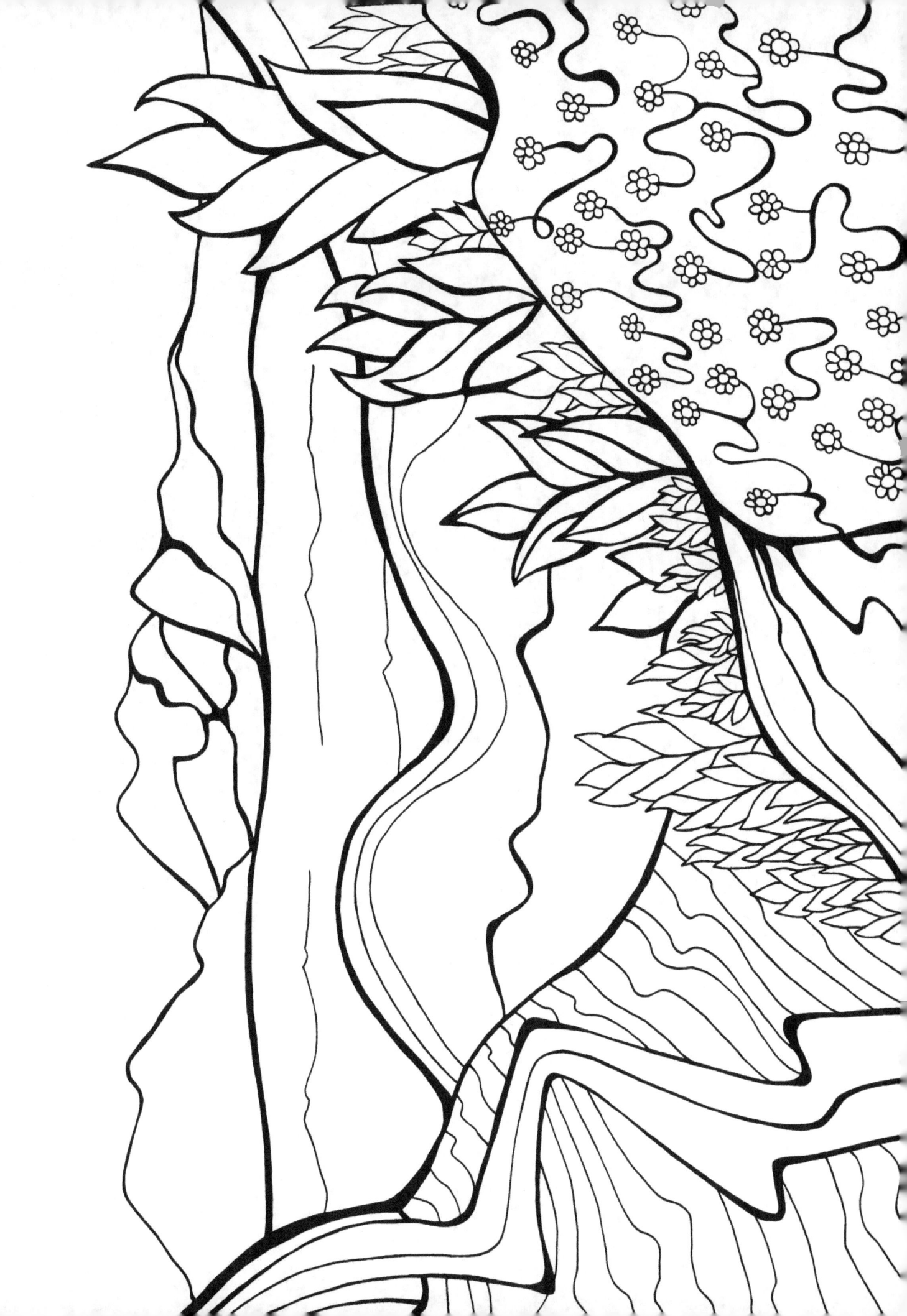

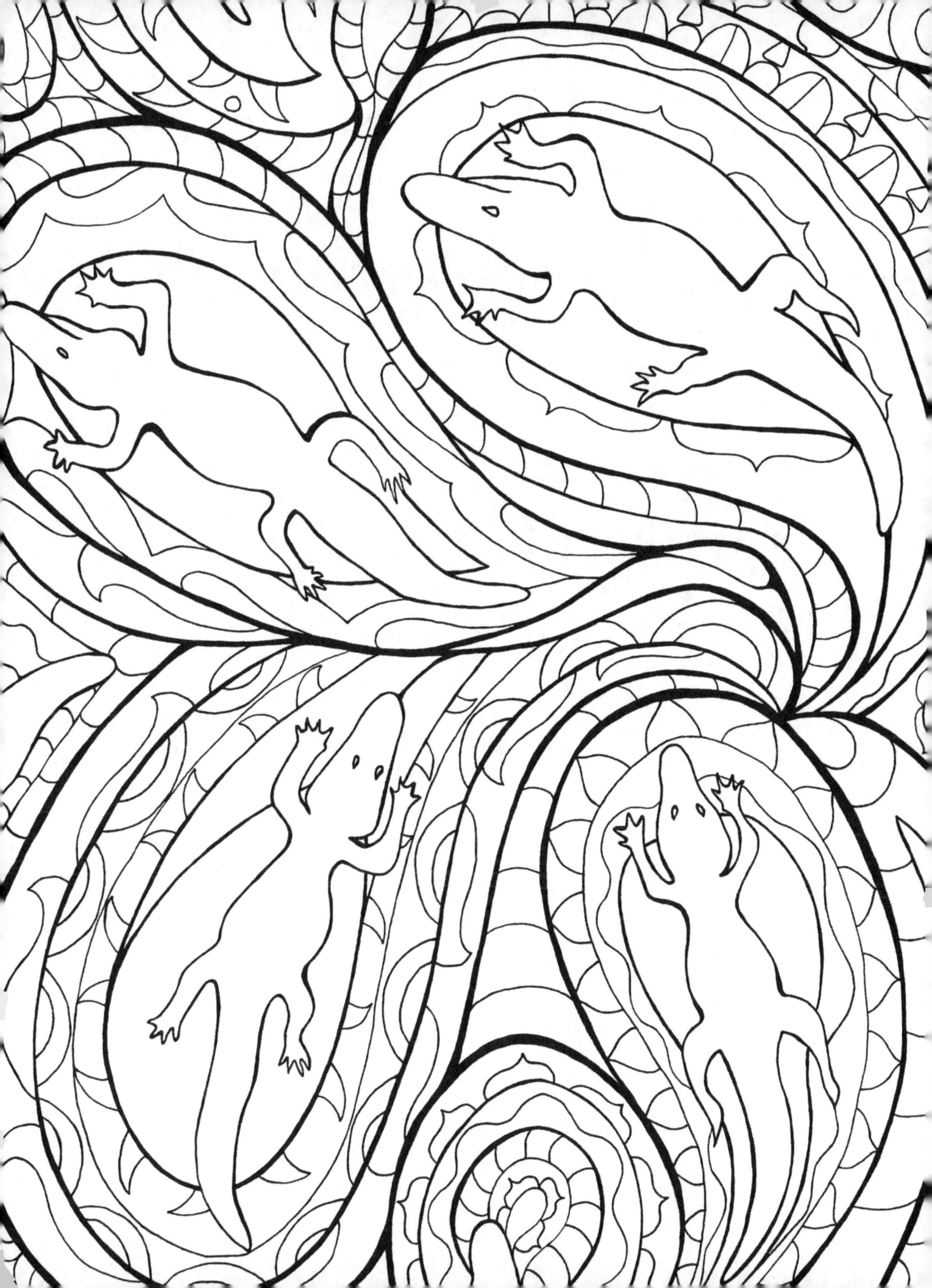

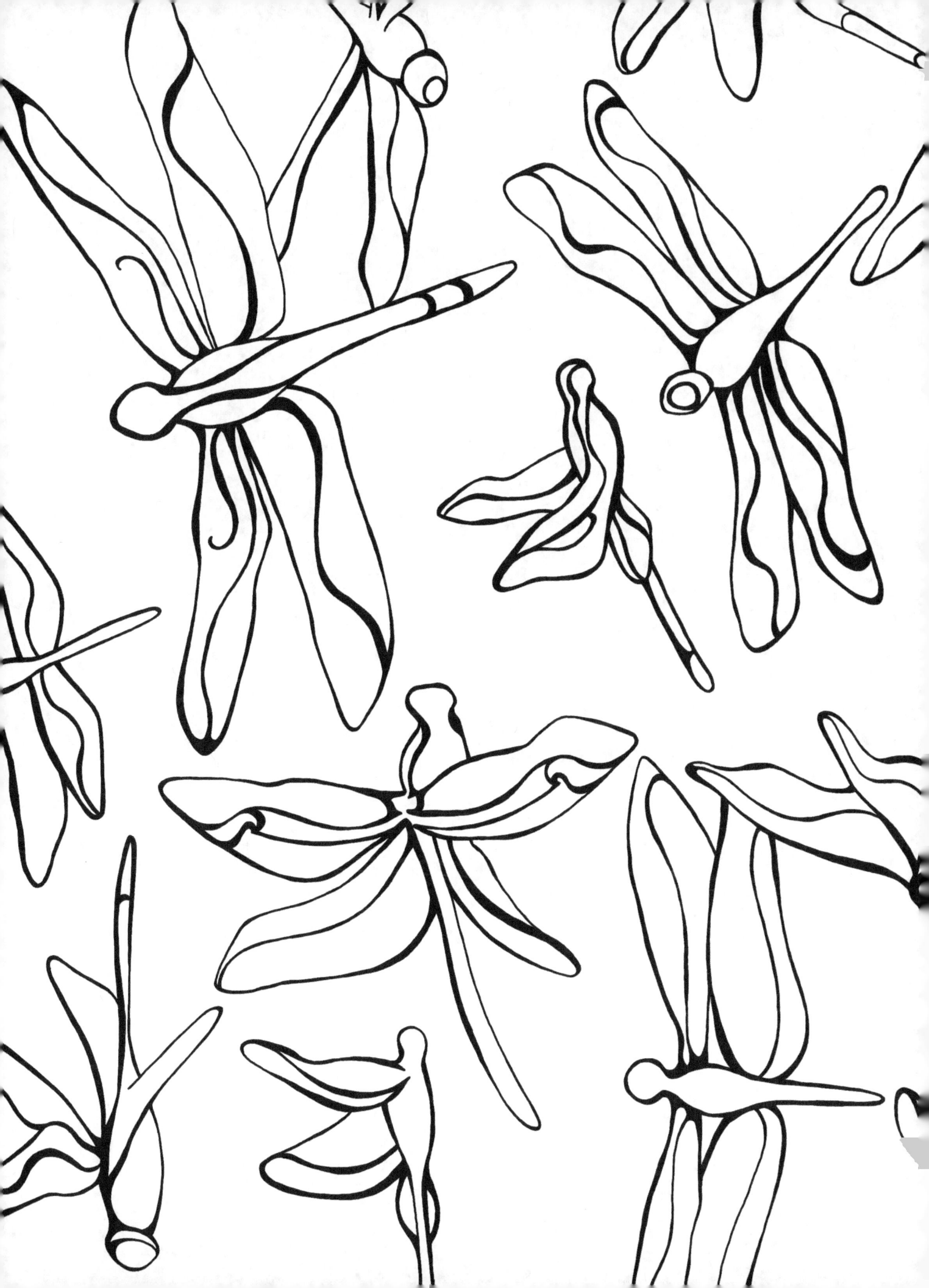

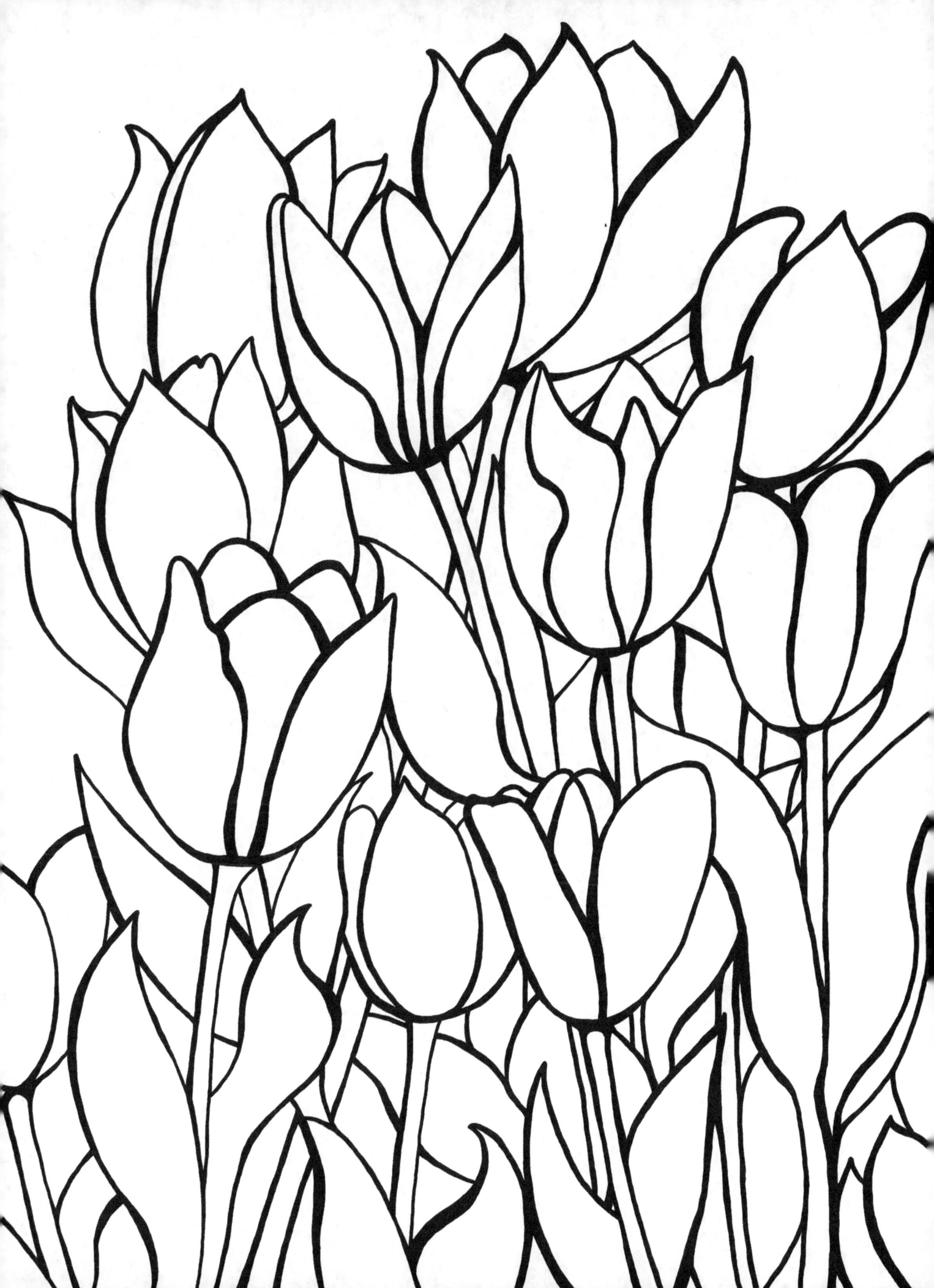

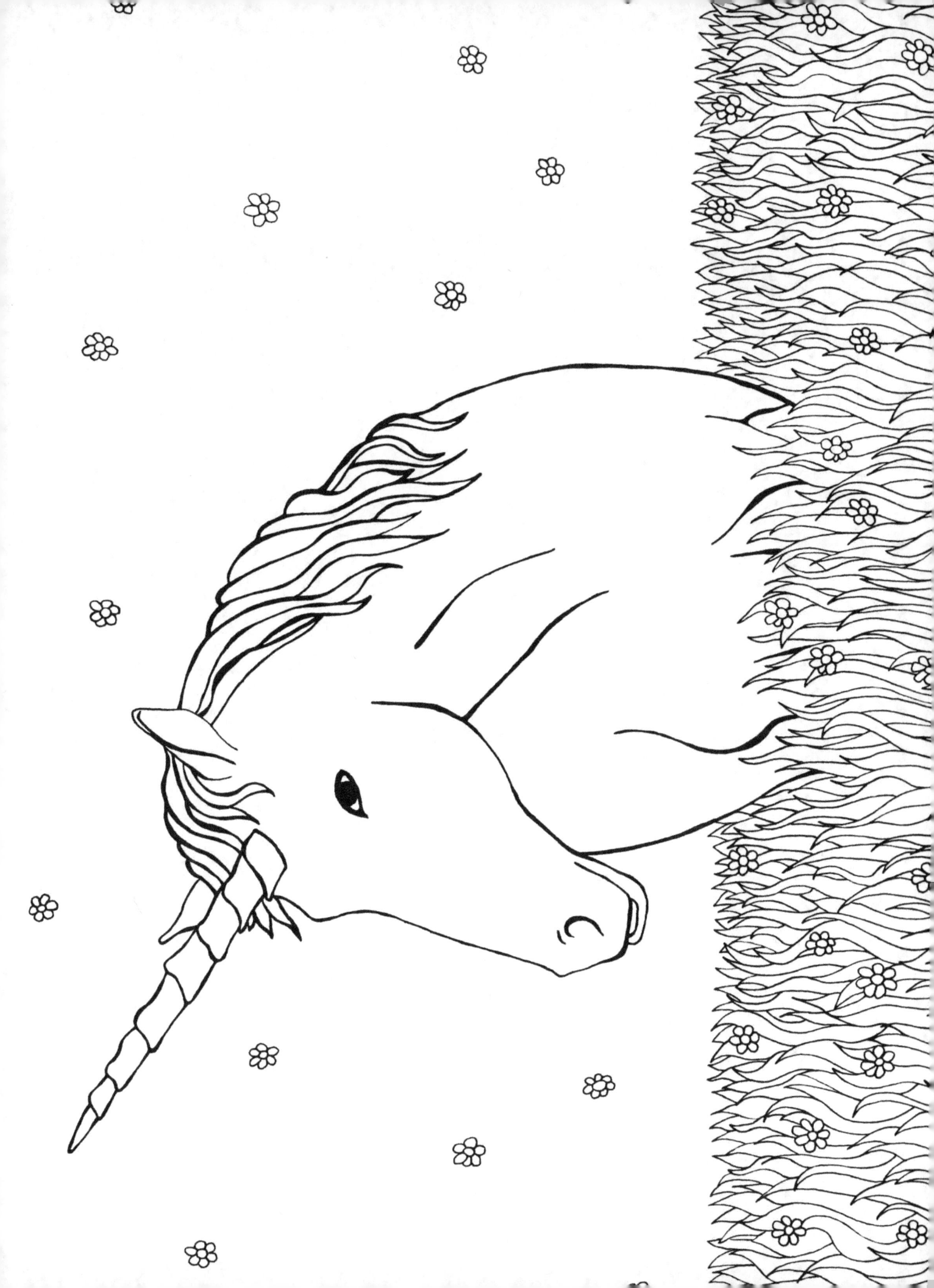

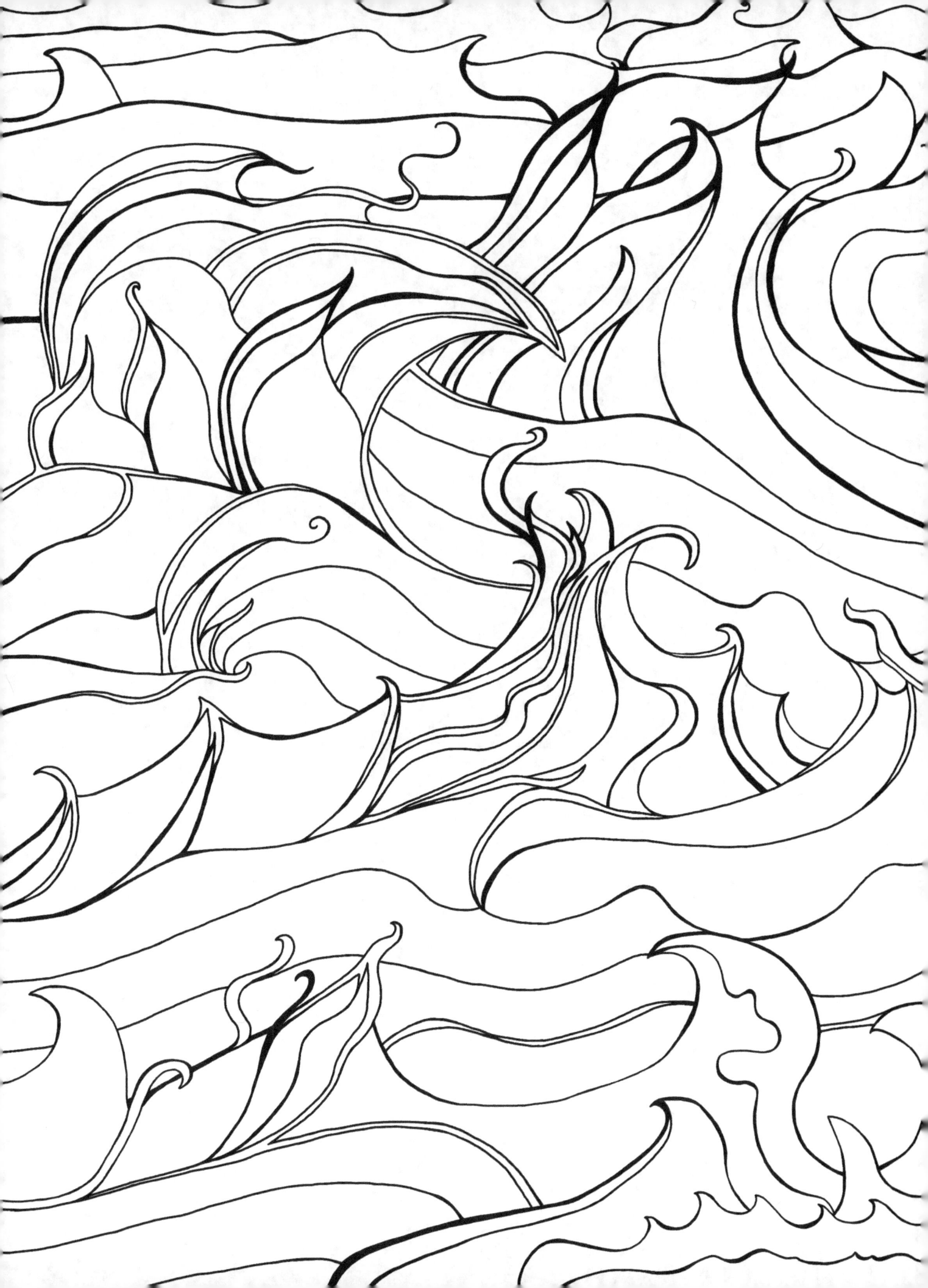

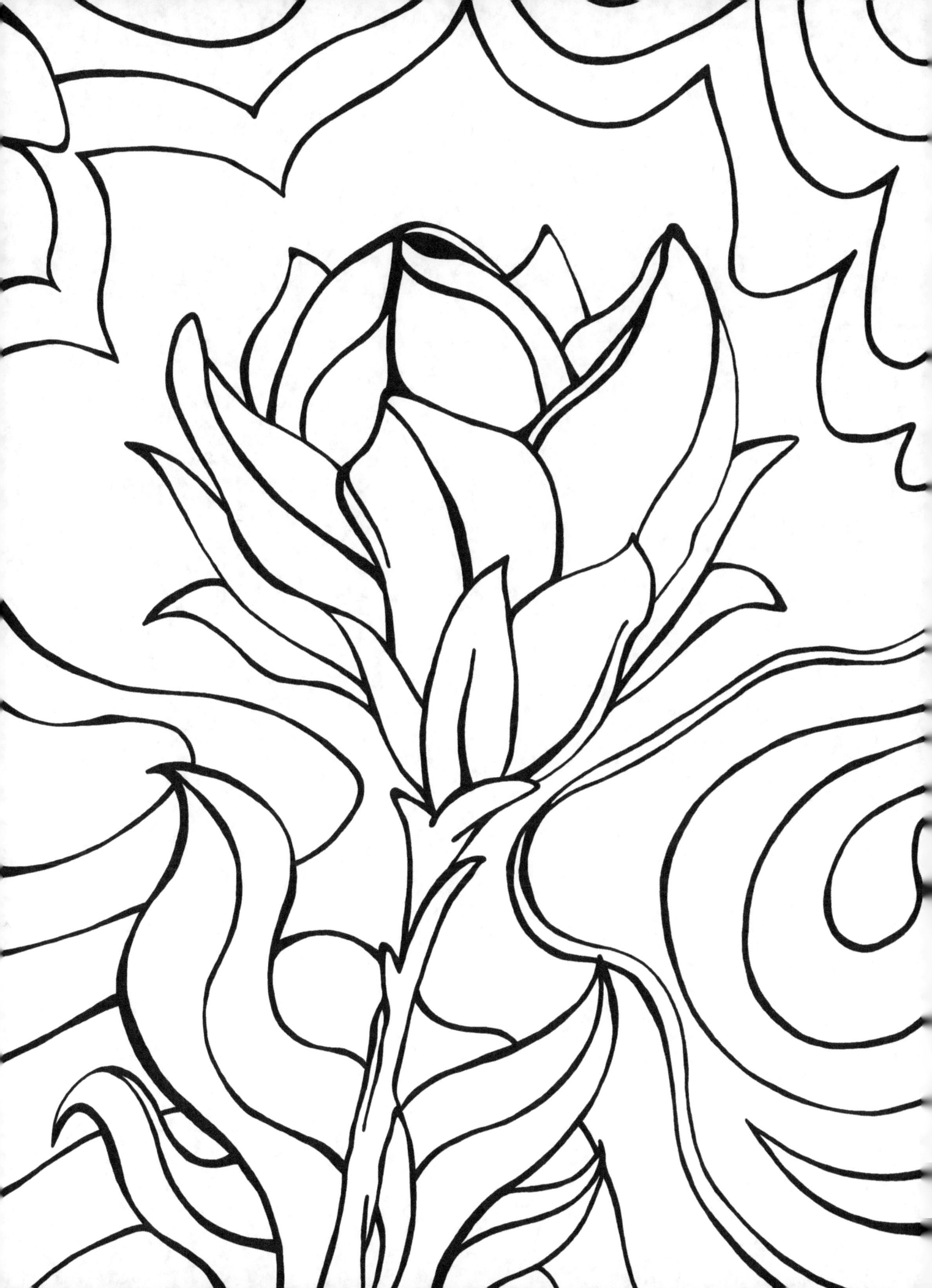

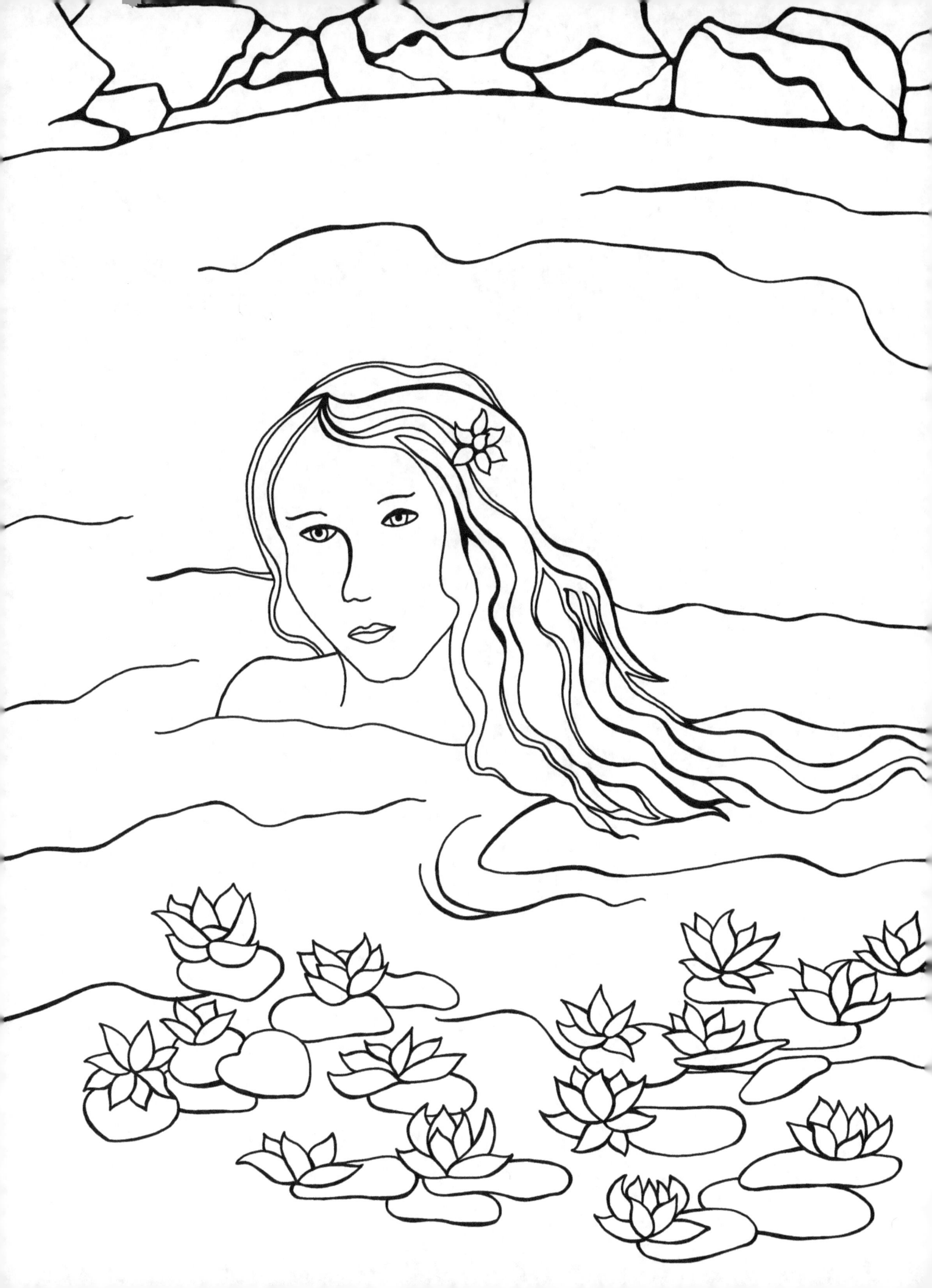

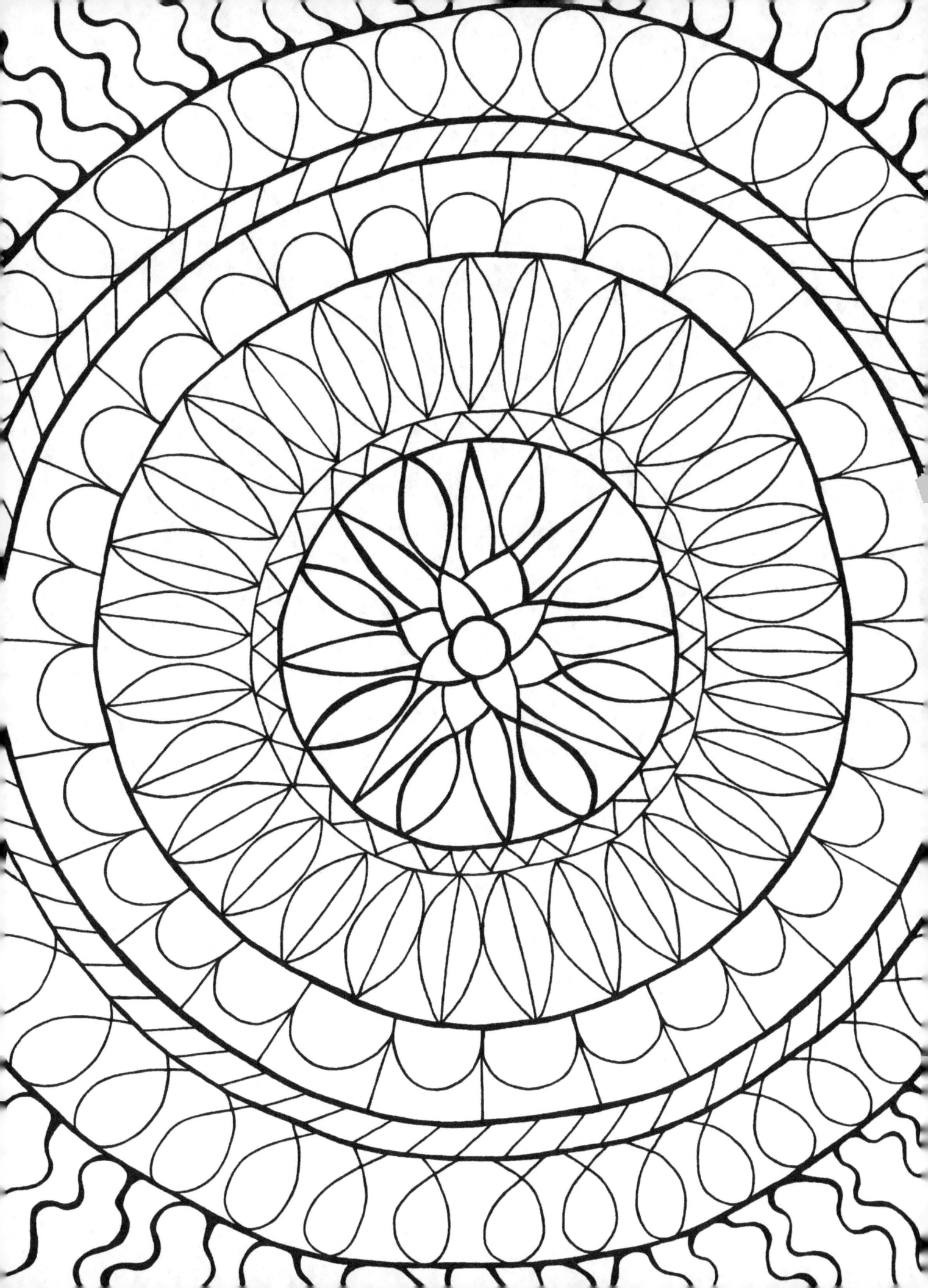

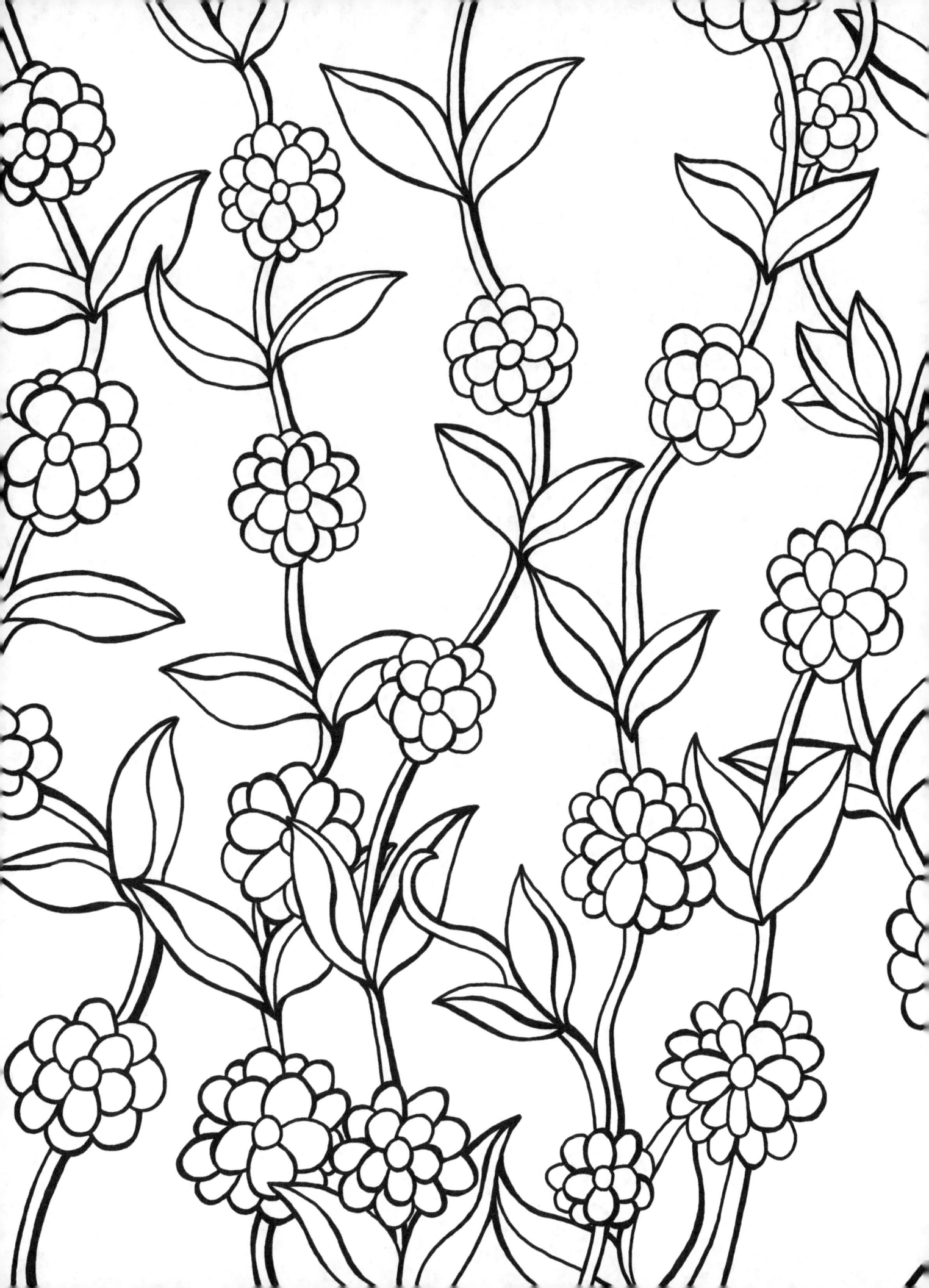

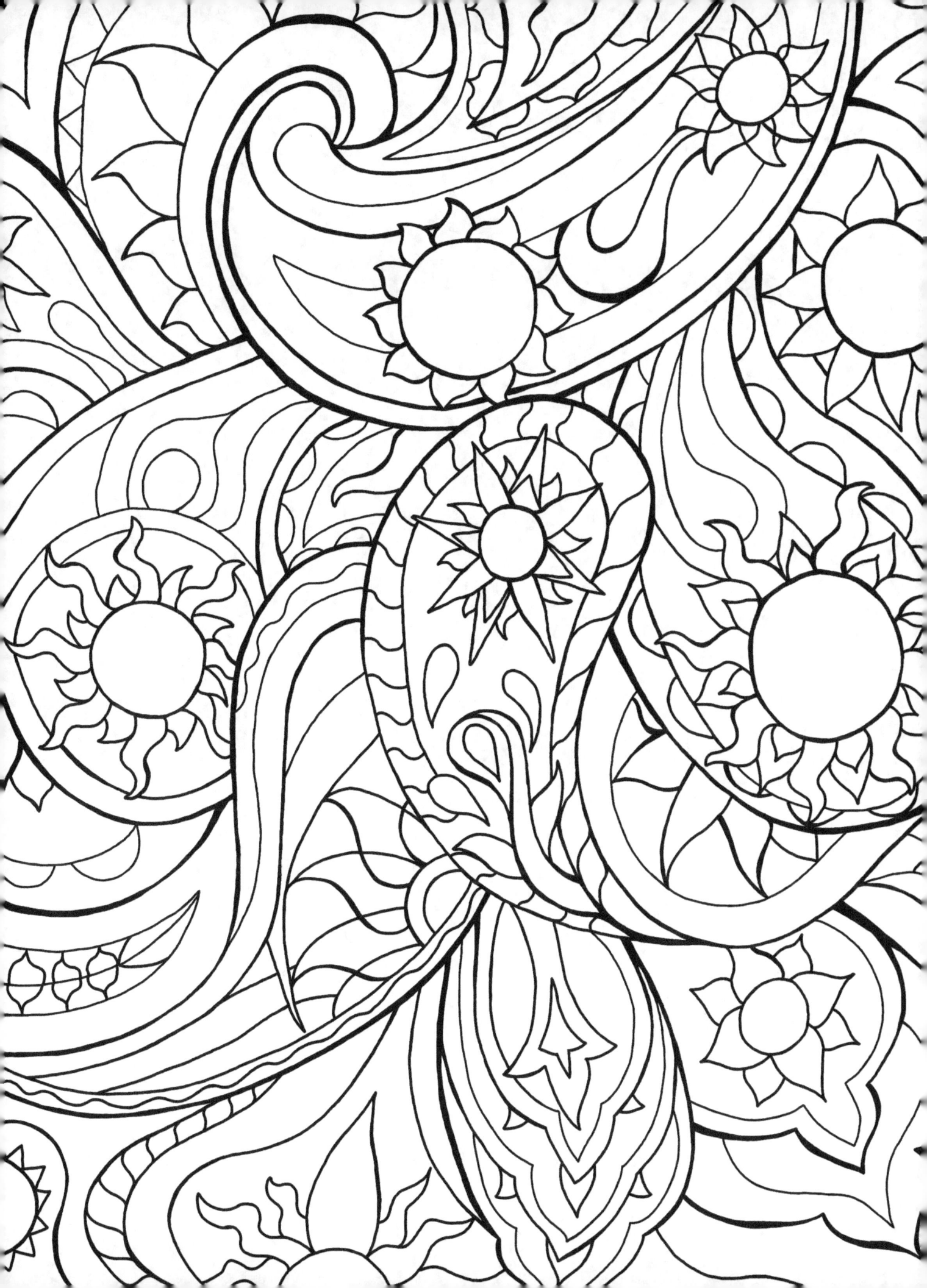

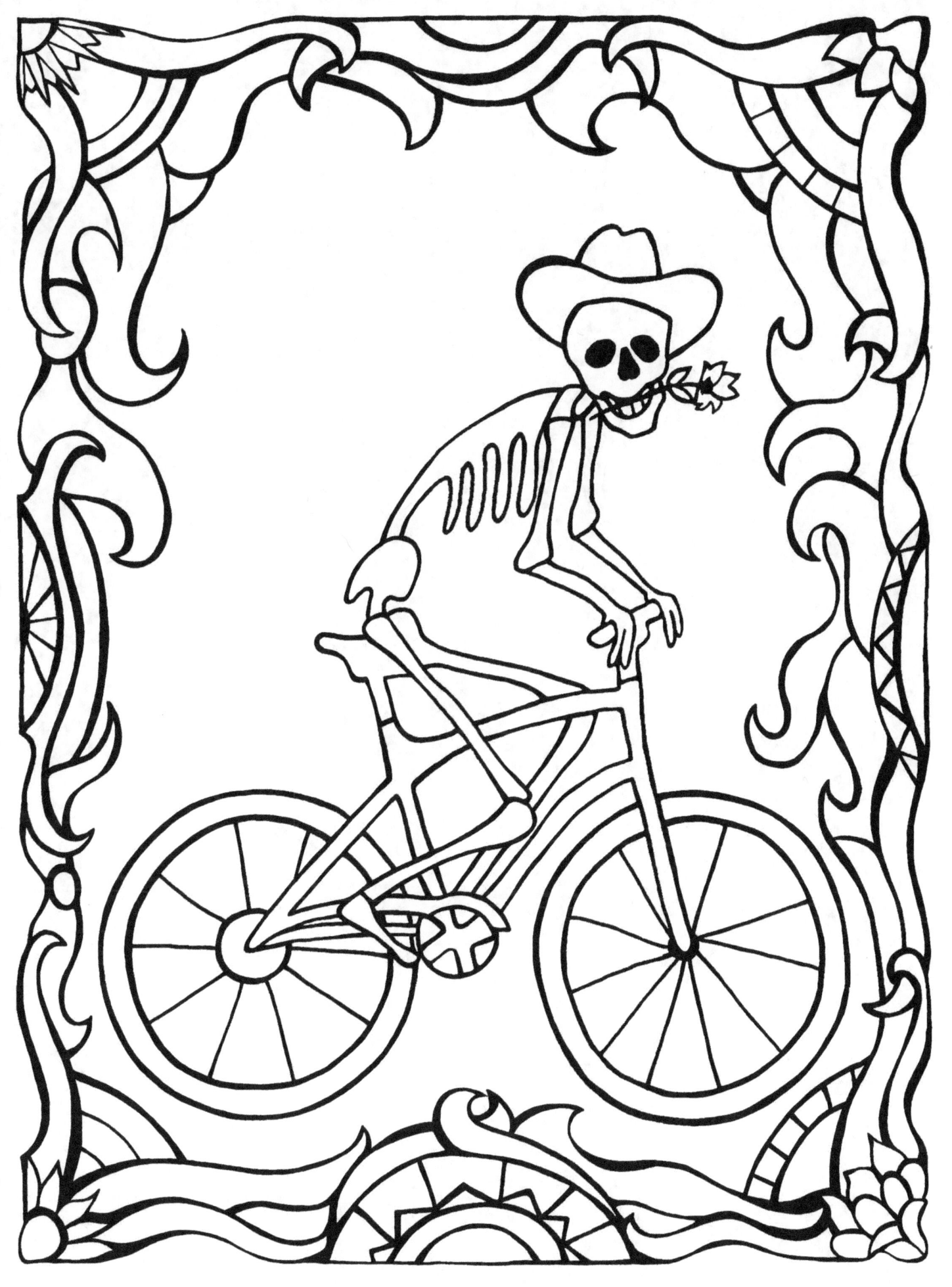

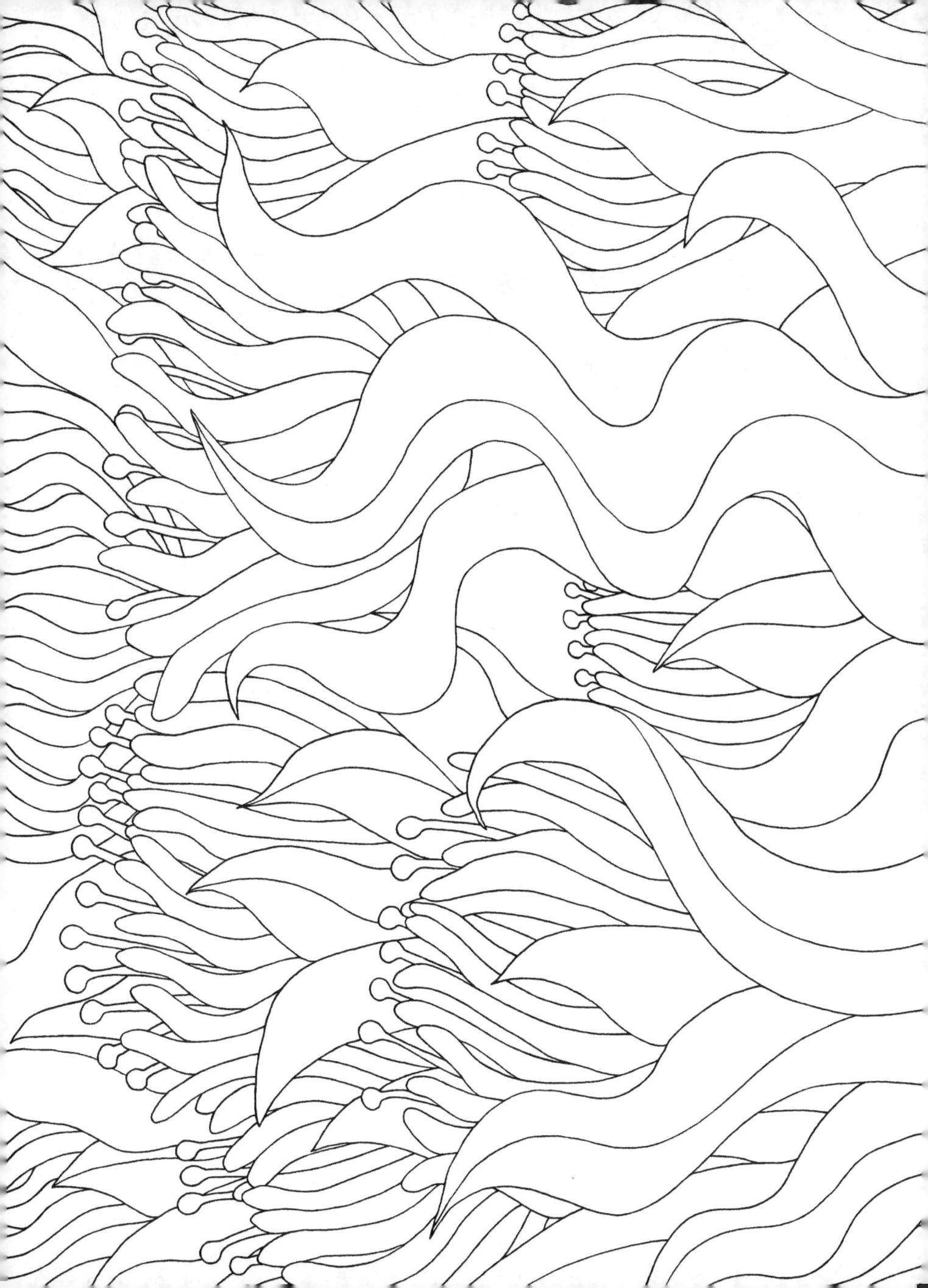

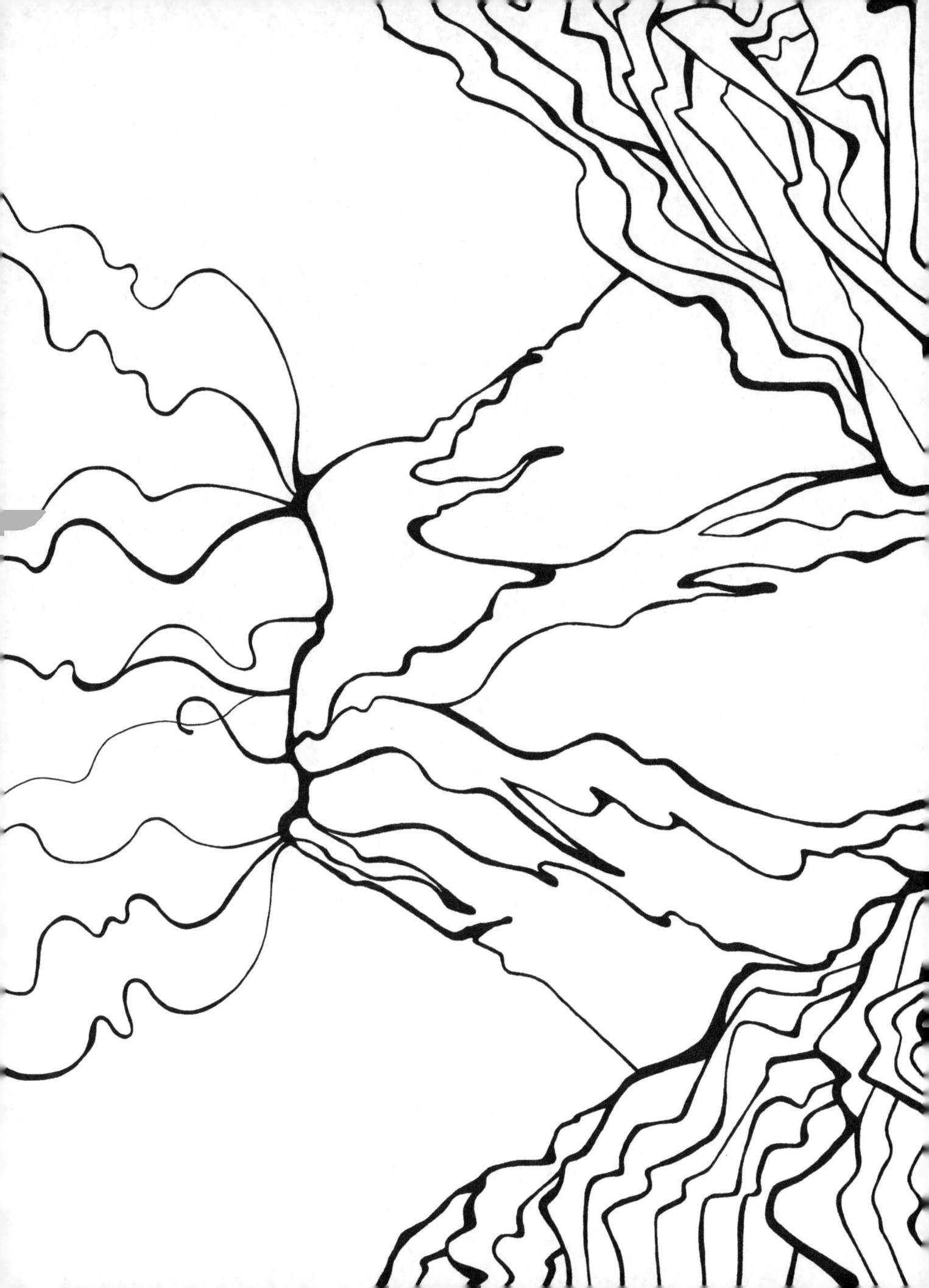

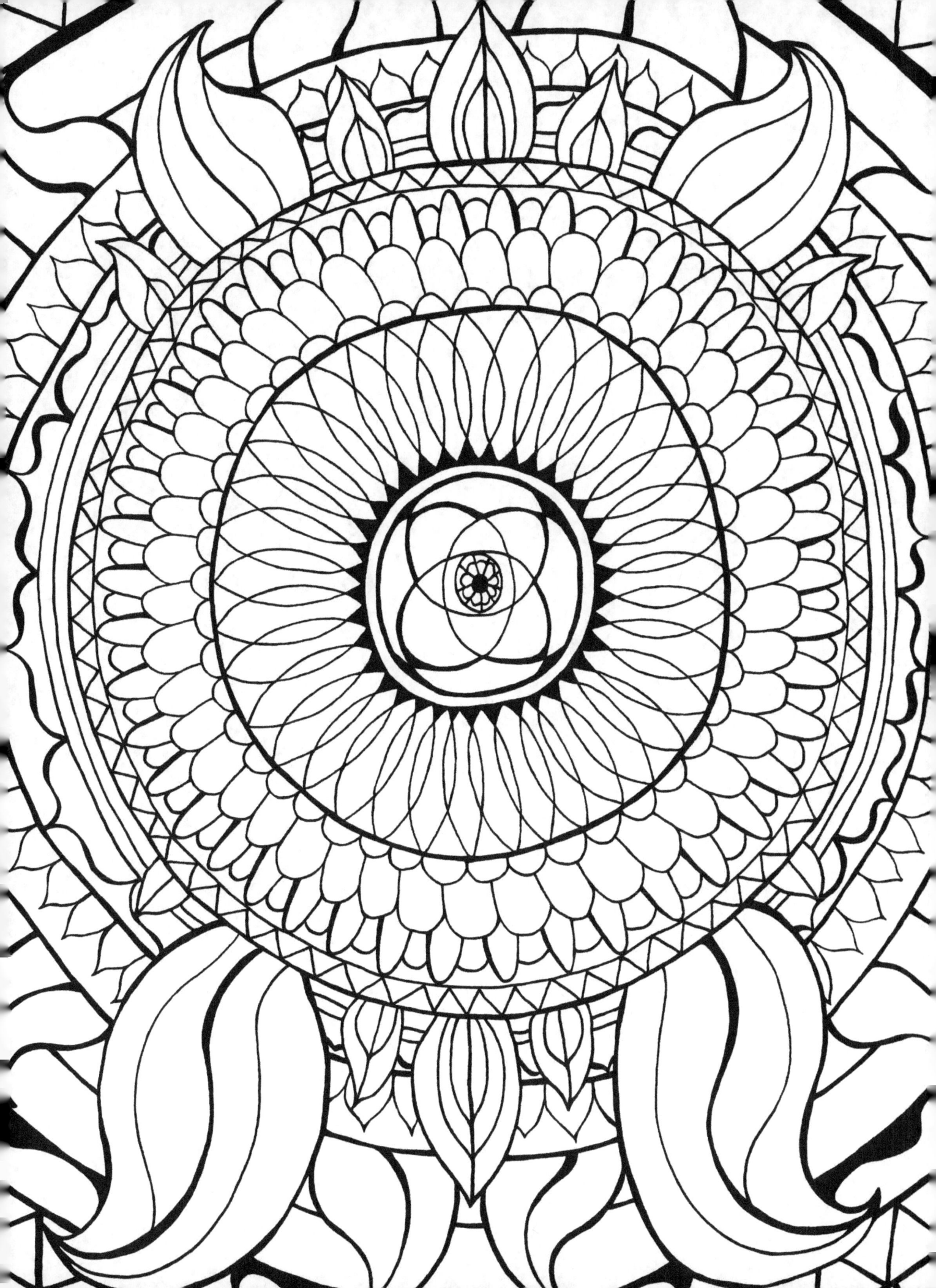

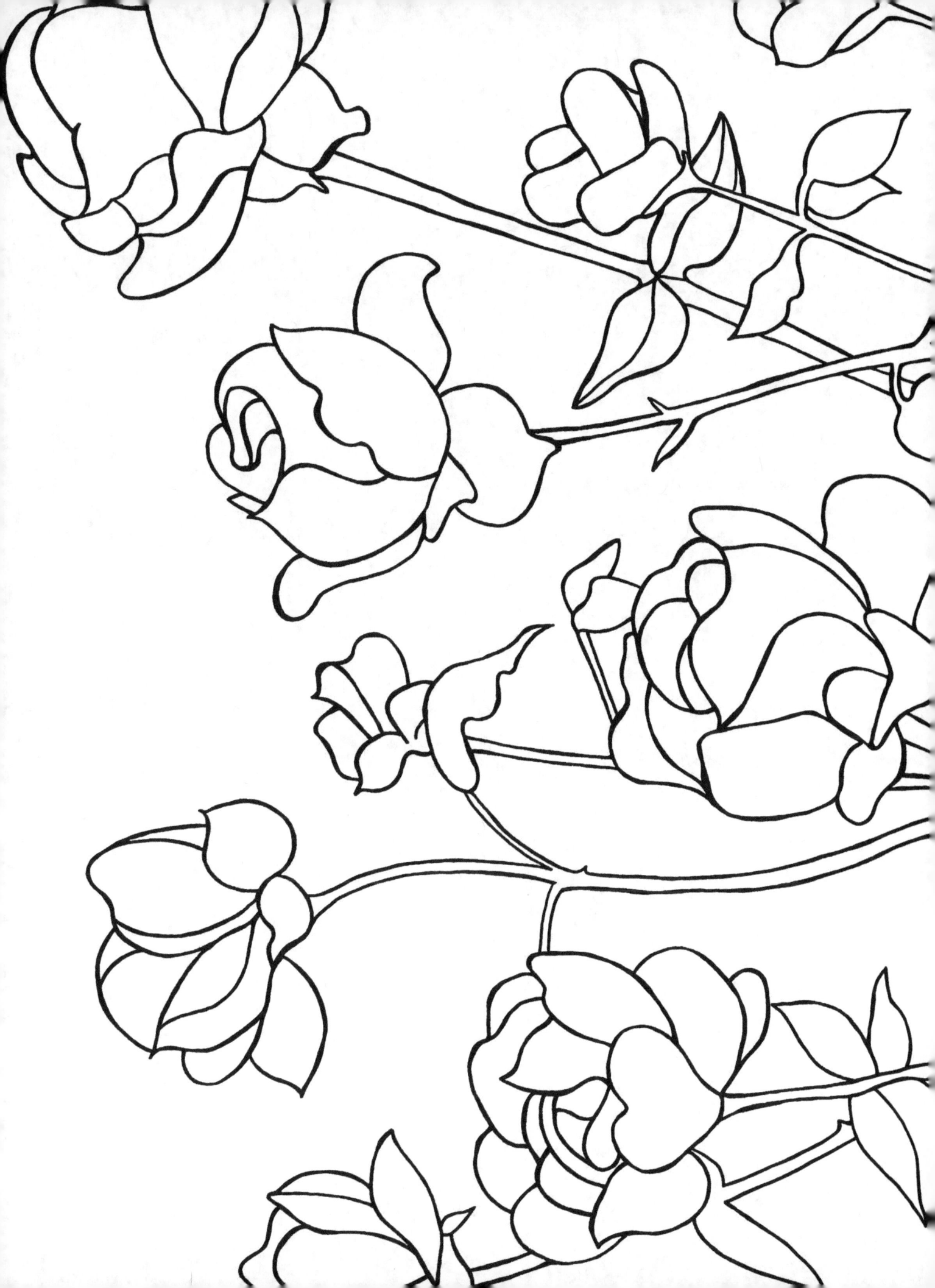

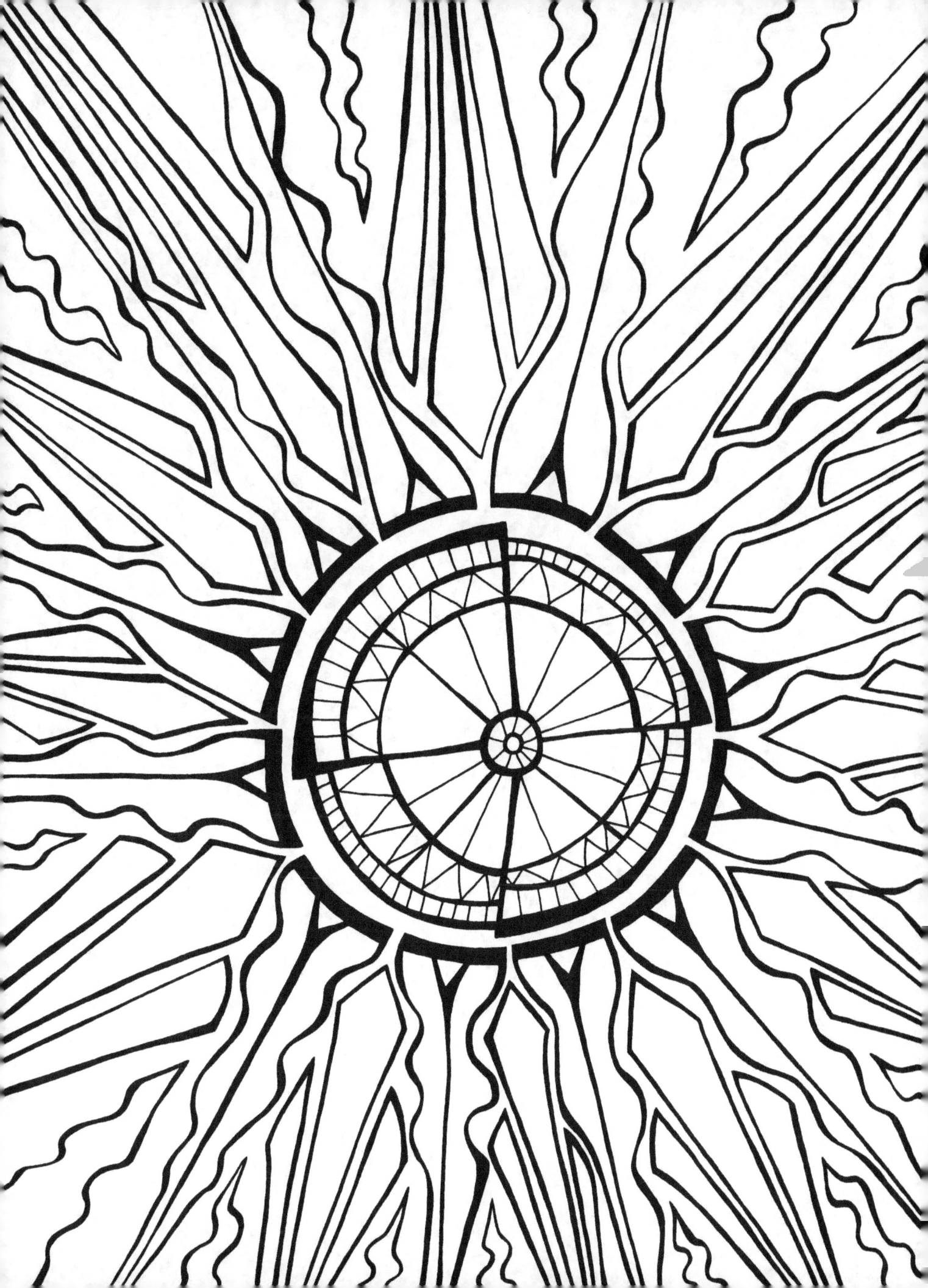

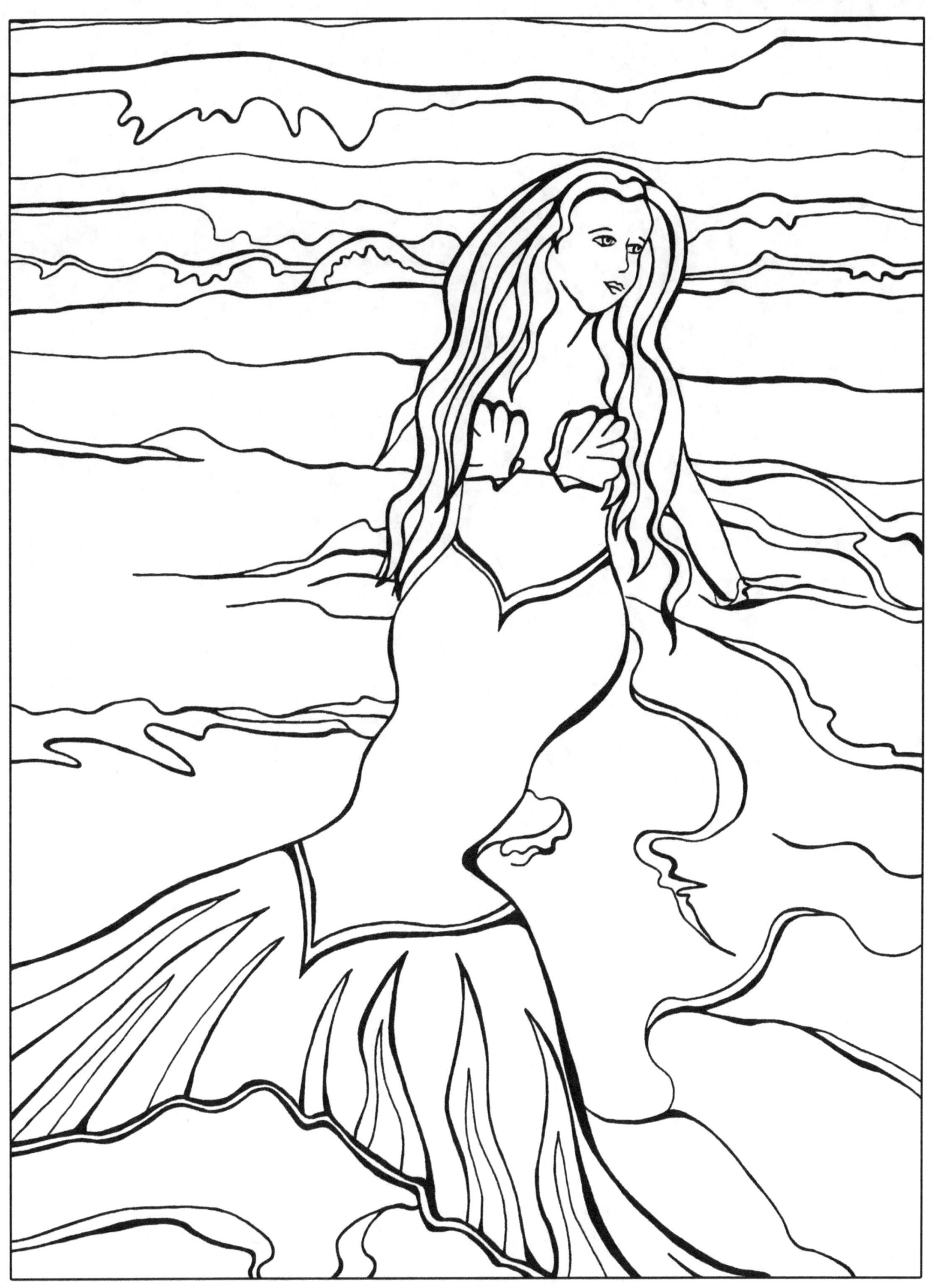

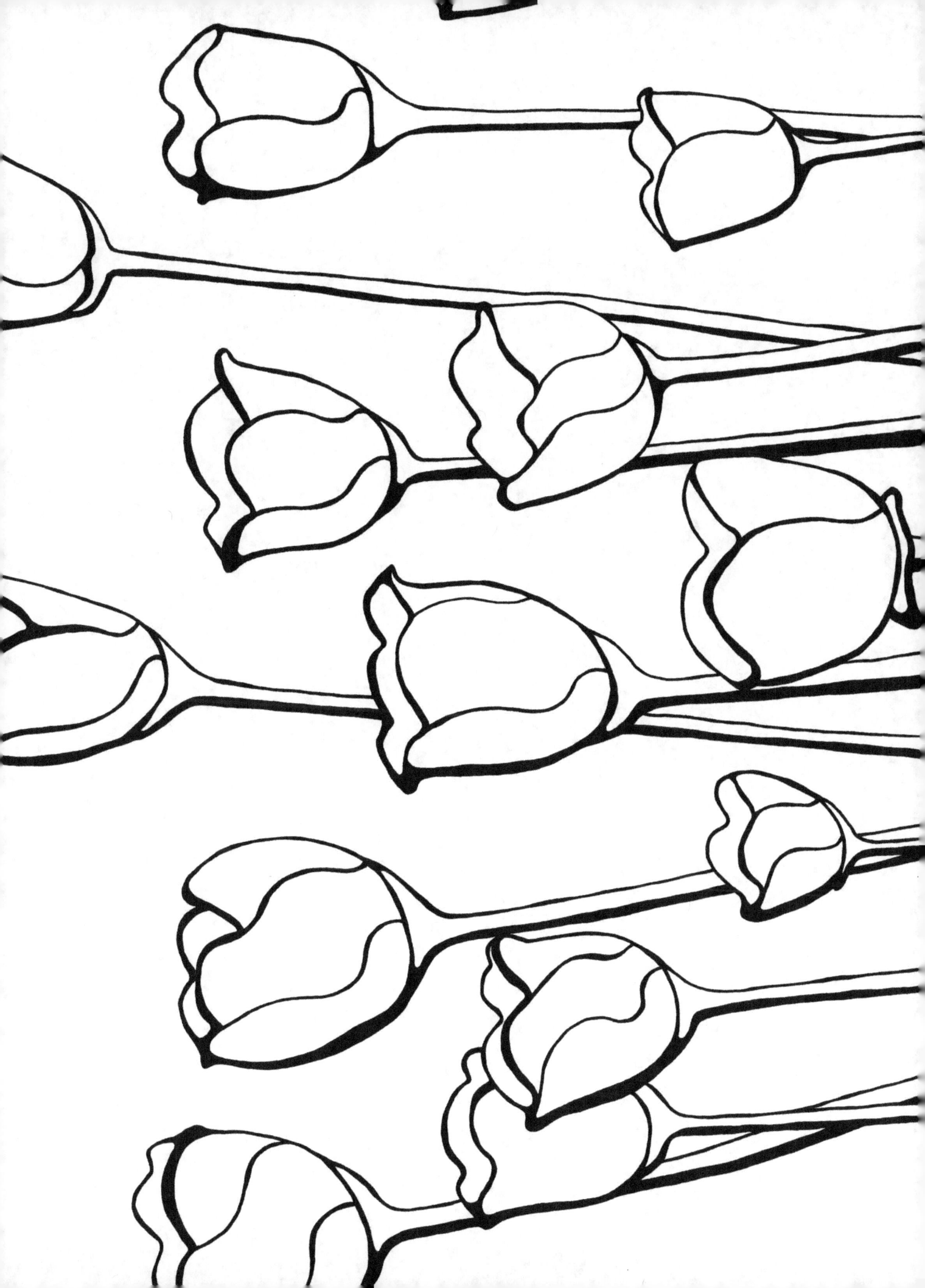

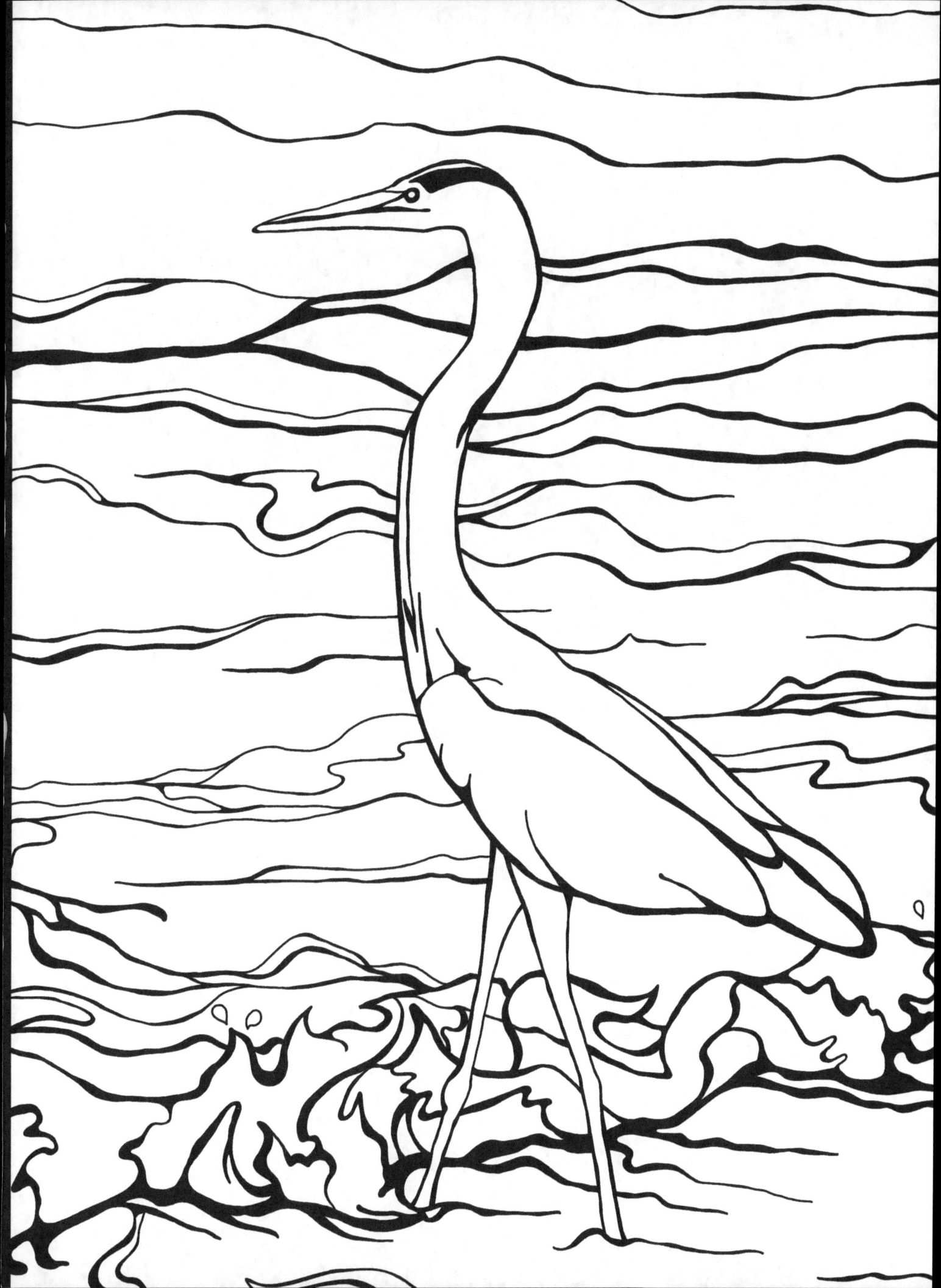

www.ingramcontent.com/pod-product-compliance
Lightning Source LLC
Chambersburg PA
CBHW080132240526
45468CB00009BA/2371